PARTNERS IN PRODUCTION?

PARTNERS IN PRODUCTION?

Women, Farm and Family in Ireland

Patricia O'Hara

Berghahn Books
NEW YORK · OXFORD

First published in 1998 by

Berghahn Books

© 1998 Patricia O'Hara

Library of Congress Cataloging-in-Publication Data
O'Hara, Patricia, 1952–
    Partners in Production? : women, farm, and family in Ireland /
Patricia O'Hara.
        p.   cm.
    Includes bibliographical references and index.
    ISBN 1-57181-939-8 (hardcover : alk. paper). -- ISBN 1-57181-969-X
(pbk. : alk. paper)
    1. Women in agriculture--Ireland. 2. Family farms--Ireland.
3. Ireland--Rural conditions.   I. Title.
HD6073.A292I736   1998
305.43'63--dc21   97-38373
                                                                CIP

British Library Cataloguing in Publication Data

A catalogue record for this book is available from the
British Library.

Cover photographs reproduced by kind permission of Hugh McElveen

For Johnny

CONTENTS

LIST OF TABLES

ACKNOWLEDGEMENTS

When I began preliminary work on this book I was a Senior Research Officer in the Rural Sociology Department of the Agricultural Institute (now incorporated into Teagasc) and my association with former colleagues has continued. Particular thanks to Patrick Commins, Head of the Rural Economy Research Unit, who facilitated access to data as well as providing intellectual stimulation and humour during the course of the research. Thanks are also due to Michael Cushion, Dan Twohig, Phonsie Comey, P.J. Burke and Tony McGarry for technical assistance. Kevin Lynch has long been my mentor in computer matters and was an invaluable guide to hardware and software. Hilary Tovey, Trinity College, Dublin provided wise intellectual advice and thoughtful and constructive criticisms at all stages of the research. Her astute sociological mind and gentle encouragement and humour were of immeasurable help in sharpening my thinking and maintaining my enthusiasm. To my parents, farm children both, I owe my curiosity about the issues in this book. My father's lifelong fascination with farming has proven to be hereditary, while my mother's stories of her own and other women's lives made me realise how much has been lost and undocumented. My thanks also to my cousin Mary MacAodha and her family for their solicitude and for many good dinners. Many friends have contributed to my thinking and my sanity over the past few years, my thanks to all and particularly to Carmel Kelleher for unwavering support and encouragement. Thanks to Pat O'Connor and Barbara Murray who read earlier drafts and provided sound advice. John Callaghan's unconditional love and support sustained me in countless ways. He acted as a sounding board for ideas and challenged me to clarify my arguments by providing invaluable comments on drafts. Above all, he never let me lose heart. With love and thanks for his enriching presence in my life and for all we have shared during its preparation, the book is dedicated to him. Finally, I hope I have done justice to the women interviewees who so generously and graciously welcomed me into their homes. Their cooperation is greatly appreciated.

1

WOMEN IN FAMILY FARMING IN IRELAND

The Context

Introduction

The family and the farm are among the most cherished institutions in Irish society and both are given special recognition in the Irish Constitution. Article 41 asserts that the family is the 'natural, primary and fundamental unit group of Society' and guarantees to protect it as 'the necessary basis of social order'. Article 45.2.v obliges the state to ensure that as many 'families' as possible are retained on the land. The importance attached to farming reflects the fact that until recent decades, Ireland[1] was predominantly an agricultural country whose people retain a strong rural identity. Even today, the majority of Irish people outside Dublin live in rural areas and, although the numbers in farming have declined consistently throughout this century, the sector remains a vital element in the national economy, accounting for thirteen percent of employment and nine percent of Gross Domestic Product (compared to the corresponding European Union averages of three percent and six percent). Virtually all farms are family enterprises; and family farming as a social form has considerable economic, social and ideological significance.

Numerical decline and the real or imagined threat of extinction have reinforced the ideological commitment to family farming as the most desirable way of organising agricultural production and ensuring the future viability of rural communities. In debates on the future of agriculture in the context of changing market conditions – such as the reform of the Common Agricultural Policy (CAP) of the European Union (EU) – its importance is frequently stressed and the alternative

1. Ireland, throughout this book, refers to the Republic of Ireland.

portrayed as 'factory farming'. In the discourse of policy and pressure groups and in official statistics, the family farm is treated as a consensual unit headed by a male farmer. Although women are the other half of the farm family, they are barely acknowledged and remain hidden in its shadows. Officially and publicly, family farming is represented by the male farmer who owns the land, represents the family in farming organisations, and is subject to taxation or entitled to social security. The women who are involved in family farming, as the wives of such males, have no independent status in the family farm and, unless they have an independent paid occupation, they are commonly thought of and referred to as farmers' wives. For this reason it is difficult even to estimate the precise number of women on Irish farms, as these women are not enumerated as a separate category in the Census of Population or in Labour Force Surveys. Like all women doing unpaid work, they are classified as 'engaged in home duties' regardless of their work input to the farm. Of course, farm wives in this sense are not the only women involved in family farming in Ireland, but they do constitute the great majority of women on family farms.

Despite their invisibility in the public world of agriculture, farm women are self-evidently at the heart of family farming which clearly involves much more than the individual male farmer/operator working his land. The process of family formation, of bearing and rearing children, through which family farming is established and continues intergenerationally, intimately involves them. In addition, many farm women contribute substantially to farm production for the market and for home consumption and, almost invariably, undertake all of the domestic work in the farm household in addition to childcare and (sometimes) eldercare. When they work off the farm, their income is often essential to the family's well-being. Through engaging in voluntary work, they make a major contribution to the quality of rural life, and they are increasingly participating in locally based rural development initiatives. Women's actions are therefore essential to the survival of family farming and to the quality of rural life, but their position in farming is distinctly different from, and unequal to, that of men. At the most fundamental level, the stem family/patrilineal system (requiring the transfer of the farm holding intact to a single successor) which prevails in Ireland, involves preference for male over female heirs to farm property. This means that most farm daughters are effectively excluded from the occupation of 'farmer'. Most women who enter farming do so not through the selection of farming as an occupation, but by marrying a farmer (although, they may of course have been raised on a farm). This means that they usually do not have ownership rights to land and, often, not even to the family home. Male monopoly of the occupation of farmer also means that the farm woman is frequently cast in the role of assistant to her husband who is perceived as 'the farmer'. Women may work on the farm and contribute significantly to farm production, but have no income of their own and no independent occupational status in social security or tax regimes. As a final indignity, their work is relegated to non-work status in official statistics.

Regardless of women's work input to the farm or their involvement in other paid work, they generally also have responsibility for childcare and domestic work. This division of labour is reinforced by ideologies and cultural traditions which legitimise what is regarded as a natural and functional division of labour. It means that on many family farms, women carry a double burden of farm and household work and, while essential to the continued survival of such farms, they are nevertheless subordinated by inequalities within families which are structured on the basis of gender. Moreover, women are conspicuously absent from (or marginalised in) the public world of farming organisations, agri-support services, agricultural cooperatives, the farming media, and many of the organisational structures associated with initiatives to promote rural development.

The assumption of the farm family as a consensual unit obscures gender as a social division within farm families. The reality is that within family farming and in the wider world of agriculture, women are apparent subordinates. They cannot therefore be assumed to have the same interests as men. Moreover, the way in which farm women perceive and deal with their subordination is likely to have a significant effect on the evolution of family farming. Little is known of how gender relations actually work themselves out within farm families, or of farm women's understanding of their situation, but even a casual observer would conclude that Irish farm women are not without influence. The sources of such influence and its effects, given their apparent subordination, are of crucial importance to understanding both the farm women's predicament and the future of family farming.

These are among the issues and concerns which underlie the research on which this book is based. They give rise to questions such as: how exactly are women involved in family farming; in what ways are they subordinated and how does this constrain them; are they helping to reproduce a patriarchal regime or are they contesting patriarchal structures in their own particular way; are they contesting and cooperating at the same time; what are the sources of their influence and how do their actions affect the future of family farming; and, since women are essential to the reproduction of family farming, are they also influencing its dissolution? Answering these questions involved investigating the nature and extent of women's involvement in family farming and its significance for the survival of this form of enterprise; examining the ways in which farm women are subordinated in daily life on the farm, including their ownership of or access to farm family assets; investigating whether or how farm women contest subordination; and, how all of this affects the reproduction of family farming. But before turning to a discussion of how these questions are addressed in this volume, it is necessary to outline the context of the research by setting out and clarifying some key aspects of family farming in Ireland, as well as referring briefly to the existing data on women's involvement in family farming.

Family Farming in Ireland

Family farming is the dominant social form in Irish agriculture and the term 'family farm' refers to individual farm holdings in family ownership, where production for the market is achieved almost exclusively through family labour. Hired labour is relatively uncommon on all but the largest Irish farms and the farm family usually resides on the holding. The term 'farm family' therefore, refers to the family living and working on the farm holding. The patrilineal system of impartible inheritance means that reproduction of the family farm as a social form is fundamentally dependent on the processes of family formation and successful transmission of the farm to the next generation. The concealment of women in family farming has been referred to already. The only Irish women with an occupational identity in farming are either those farming in their own right (usually widows or single women) or female 'relatives assisting' on farms. In the 1991 Census of Population, 6,800 women classified themselves as farmers in their own right, the majority of these being widows or single women. A further 5,900 women were counted as relatives assisting on farms (Central Statistics Office, 1994a). Together they represent just under ten percent of all those enumerated on farms. The strongly patrilineal nature of family farming is reflected in the fact that there were just sixty-five farm daughters/daughters-in-law enumerated as working on farms, compared to 11,100 farm sons/sons-in-law. The remainder of women on family farms then are the wives of male 'farmers' and, although the term 'farmer' is not always unambiguous, it is usually taken to mean the male operator of the farm holding.[2] Women on farms in this wife/mother role (the female half of the couple

2. For a more detailed account of these problems of definition, see the section on farm wives' official invisibility in Chapter Five.

who comprise the nuclear farm family) are the primary focus of this book, hence my use of the term 'farm wife' as well as farm woman.

The 1991 Census of Agriculture[3] (Central Statistics Office, 1994b) provided the first real estimate of the numbers of 'farm wives' on Irish farms when farm family labour was disaggregated on the basis of sex and marital status for the first time, including women who were involved in 'farm work'. According to this Census there were 91,400 female family members on family farms in Ireland. Of these, more than two thirds (70 percent) were the spouses of the farm holder. Almost three quarters of farm wives (74 percent) had farming as their sole or major occupation. These data provide only a relatively crude estimation of women's involvement in Irish farming as the assumptions and definitions of 'work' on which they are based are quite restricted. They do however give us some appreciation of the relative scale of the population of 'farm wives' in Irish farming.

Family farms in Ireland are comparatively small in scale with sixty percent of farms being classified as small or relatively small.[4] Dairying, cattle, sheep and tillage are the main farming systems. Farming has undergone major changes in the last four decades, and particularly in the years since entry to the EU (then the EEC) in 1973. These changes have been characterised by increased use of technology, scale enlargement, and specialisation involving considerable expansion in output and incomes from farming. This restructuring has led to widening differences between farm size groups, systems of farming and regions. Production has become concentrated on a minority of larger farms which are commercial in orientation, comparatively efficient and relatively prosperous. These farms are overwhelmingly located in the east and south of the country and on good quality land. The trend towards specialisation has resulted in the more lucrative systems such as dairying and tillage predominating on larger farms in the east, while low-intensity livestock farming is more typical of smallholdings in the west and northwest. The smaller holdings, which comprise a majority of all farms, account for a decreasing share of aggregate output and income and commonly rely on non-farm sources of income to supplement their earnings from agriculture (Commins and Keane, 1994). Off-farm work has been crucial in allowing smallholders to continue in farming. According to the 1994 National Farm Survey (Power and Roche, 1995), one third of

3. This was the first full Census of Agriculture to be conducted in Ireland since 1980. The survey questionnaire was completed by enumerators so that, unlike the Census of Population of the same year, it was not a self-completed survey.

4. Less than eight European Size Units (ESUs). The ESU is a the standard measure of the economic size of a farm used in European Union statistics.

farm holders and/or their spouses had an off-farm job, with a higher incidence of off-farm occupations among the smaller farms. Indeed Hannan and Commins (1992: 84–85) have pointed out that farmers have been particularly adept at capturing the limited employment opportunities available in rural areas. Studies of 'pluriactive' farmers (e.g., Higgins, 1983) have shown that they are likely to be married and to be in the early to middle stages of the family life-cycle. Either spouse may be working off the farm, but the generation of off-farm income is crucial to the family's livelihood.

Although there has been a continual decline throughout this century in the numbers of those classified occupationally as farmers, there has not been a commensurate decline in the number of landholders. There is little evidence of significant consolidation of farm land. What has emerged in recent years however is a pattern of disengagement, either to part-time farming or retirement, while the land is retained by the holder (Hannan and Commins, 1993). Thus, family farming on smallholdings has remained intact but with a different orientation from that in the more commercial farming areas where a market-led logic prevails. Clearly then, there is considerable differentiation within the farming sector in Ireland and we would expect the size of the farm operation, the system of farming, and the nature and extent of off-farm work activities to be among the factors that are likely to affect the social organisation of the farm family and women's involvement in the family farm. Indeed, these are some of the themes which have been prominent in research on women in family farming over the past two decades.

Women in Family Farming

While farm women may remain largely invisible in official statistics, they have (albeit belatedly) received considerable attention from rural sociologists and agricultural economists in various countries in recent years. Many of these studies have concentrated on the gender division of labour on family farms, with the more orthodox approaches adopting a fairly narrow definition of family labour. This usually meant confining the scope of the research to documenting farm women's non-domestic work, pointing out in particular the way this labour is under-represented in official statistics (for the U.S. see Boulding, 1980; Jones and Rosenfeld, 1981; Salant, 1983; Sachs, 1983; Reimer, 1986; for England see Buchanan et al., 1982; Gasson, 1980a, 1980b, 1989; for New Zealand and Australia see Keating and Little, 1994; Alston, 1995). However localised and modest in scope, many of these empirical studies have provided important (if partial) data on women's involvement in farming and how it is changing. More recently, broader based studies of changes in farming structures have also paid some attention to women's involvement. For instance, a 1987 study of some six thousand farm households across twenty areas in the EU (including two in Ireland), revealed that forty-nine percent of farm wives were working regularly on the farm. Thirteen percent of farm operators in the formal, legal sense were women, and the vast majority of these were actively running their farms. The presence of young children and the size of the farm operation seemed to have only a minor effect on women's work. Fourteen percent of farm wives were engaged in off-farm work, with lower participation rates in the poorer areas of the EU reflecting the weakness of local labour markets (Bell et al., 1990). In England, Gasson (1992) has shown that most farm wives are involved in the farm business and that their work input is very significant, particularly on small and medium-sized holdings where there is no hired labour. Similar levels of engagement have been found in France (Berlan Darque, 1988), Spain (Garcia-Ramon and Canoves, 1988) and Switzerland (Rossier, 1993) where farm women are involved particularly in the more labour-intensive systems such as dairying. Many wives are responsible for farm book-keeping and accounts and the administrative aspects of the farm operation. Modern farming can be a complex business, requiring considerable financial management and business skills. Women frequently take on this administrative role, in many cases because they had acquired the necessary skills in a pre-marriage occupation (Symes and Marsden, 1983). In The Netherlands, Bauwens and Loeffen (1983) found that 88 percent of Dutch farm wives took part in work on the farm. They worked an average of twenty-two hours per week, the work input varying seasonally. In a more recent study of 662 full-time farms in Switzerland, Rossier (1993) found that Swiss farm women spend an average of twenty hours per week on farm work. Research on part-time farmers in Ireland revealed that more than half (56 percent) of their wives worked on the family farm, contributing an average of forty-one weeks of labour per year (Higgins, 1983).

Other studies have focused on changing gender roles associated with agricultural modernisation and the increase in pluriactivity among farm families (Bouquet, 1984; Stratigaki, 1988; Blanc and MacKinnon, 1990; Repassy, 1991; Symes, 1991; Gasson and Winter, 1992). It has been suggested that part-time farming has led to the feminisation of agricultural production in Germany, as farm wives take over more and more of the farm chores when husbands take off-farm employment (Pfeffer, 1989). DeVries (1990), on the other hand, argues that pluriactivity in the Netherlands has not increased the farm workload of women.

Almas and Haugen (1988) contend that in Norway farming has become 'masculinised' as mechanisation has reduced the need for women's labour, and employment opportunities for women in rural areas have allowed them to take up off-farm work. Stratigaki (1988) found that in Crete, commercialisation of agriculture has further confined women to the domestic sphere. Rossier (1993), in Switzerland, discovered that farm mechanisation did not lessen women's workload but the nature of the workload changed as women took on tasks formerly reserved for men. Official reports which have addressed the status of farm and rural women from a policy perspective have also pointed to the dearth of information on farm women and on the relationships between the structures of family farming and farm women's subordinate status (for Ireland see Second Commission on the Status of Women, 1993; Report of the Fourth Joint [Parliamentary] Committee on Women's Rights, 1994; for Europe see Braithwaite, 1994; European Parliament, 1994).

These studies have provided much needed information about the significance of the work of women on family farms and how it is changing. However, they have been largely uninformed by the insights of feminist analysis or the sociology of the family. By focusing on the farm rather than the farm family, they obscure the very complex set of relations which underlie the gender division of labour, and particularly the nature and distinctiveness of women's influence on the evolution of family farming as a social form. By explaining women's labour involvement in terms of family life-cycle, farming system or pluriactivity, such studies 'naturalise' the division of labour in farm households and tell us little about the social relations within the household (Whatmore, 1991).

In Ireland, while few studies have had farm women as the focus of analysis (see O'Hara 1987a, 1990; Duggan, 1987; Shortall, 1992), the farm family itself has received quite a lot of attention. Much of this work was stimulated by Arensberg and Kimball's (1940/1968) classic study of Irish farm families in the 1930s which provided a detailed account of a highly segregated gender division of labour and family interaction on peasant farms in which women were clearly subordinate. Their research also provided the starting point for Hannan and Katsiaouni's (1977) study of farm families in which they examined the task and decision-making involvement of farm husbands and wives in order to establish changes in family interaction patterns since Arensberg and Kimball's time. These works will be referred to in later chapters but there are two points about them which are worth making here. Firstly, both Arensberg and Kimball's ethnography and Hannan and Katsiaouni's perceptive analysis provide very important insights into the internal workings of the families of smallholders in the west of Ireland at two different time periods – one just a decade after the foundation of the Irish state, and the other while Ireland was in the throes of modernisation in the 1970s. Secondly, it is unfortunate that there are no comparable studies of family life among the larger more commercial farmers of the east and south. The absence of such analyses has had the effect of making the Arensberg and Kimball or Hannan and Katsiaouni farm families appear to be the norm for all Irish farming families whereas in fact both of these studies were specific to the west of Ireland. However, as we have seen, there are quite distinct east/west differences in the evolution of family farming in Ireland, so farm families from areas in both the east and west were selected for the present study.

Women's Involvement in Family Farming – The Present Study

Analyses of the evolution and future of family farming and the discourse surrounding them are largely based on unitary concepts of the farm family. It is as if only the actions of 'farmers' (who are predominantly male) affect the shape and form of family farming. At the same time, studies of women's involvement in family farming have mainly focused on women's work roles in relation to the farming enterprise or their subordination by the gendered structures of family farming. Women emerge from such studies as relatively powerless and without influence, but such a view of Irish farm women is contradicted by even casual empirical observation. While family farming as a social form is undoubtedly patriarchal, and farm women remain hidden in the shadows of the farm family, Irish women have long resisted the constraints of family farming. Farm daughters have for decades migrated out of rural areas in large numbers, often to the cities of North America or Britain, and eschewed rural life and marriage to farmers. Those who did become farm wives and mothers have had a profound but little understood influence on the evolution of Irish society, perhaps better articulated in Irish fiction (drama and prose) than in scholarly discourse. This brings us to the starting point for this study in which I set out to investigate farm women's distinct and separate influence on the evolution of family farming, and how this is related to their apparent subordinate status on family farms. In undertaking the research I was concerned to uncover women's place in family farming in Ireland not only to redress years of neglect and androcentric bias in research and statistics, but also because the significance of gender as a social division within farm families has received little attention in the context of contemporary concerns about the future of family farming and the associated continued viability of rural areas.

The theoretical orientation adopted in the research sought to widen the compass of conceptual approaches to understanding women's involvement in family farming by bringing together debates about the future of family farming, feminist theories of women's work and the sociology of the family. Drawing on concepts and ideas from these discourses, I argue that understanding the situation of farm women involves looking inside both the family farm *and* the farm family. Each must be deconstructed in order to explore and understand women's place in them. While the constraints associated with the patriarchal structures of family farming are clearly acknowledged and investigated, farm women are conceptualised as active agents, constructing and shaping the world around them. In this way their distinct experience of family farming and their influence on the evolution of this social form and on Irish society can become apparent. This means that power is conceptualised, not in an absolutist way, but as a negotiated process, often informal and unarticulated. The position taken is that there is always room to manoeuvre and that the sources of women's power and influence are intertwined with their responses to subordination.

In practice, the study investigated not just women's experience of life on the family farm and the nature of the work that they do, but also examined the way in which the distribution of resources within farm families is structured on the basis of gender. It also included a major focus on farm wives' involvement in reproduction in order to comprehend the way in which their actions shape the evolution of family farming and how this is related to their responses to the constraints of patriarchal structures. Thus, in addition to production, the study investigated areas hitherto largely unexplored in studies of family farming – consumption and reproduction. Analysis of farm wives' involvement in production and consumption reveals the nature and extent of their subordination and the way in which they resist the constraints of patriarchal structures, culture and ideology by fashioning their own spheres of influence through, for instance, changing and shaping new ideologies of marriage and family, or retaining their pre-marriage occupations in order to strengthen their negotiating power in family relationships. However, it is in their reproductive role that we find the most significant, and hitherto largely ignored, source of farm women's power. As mothers, who bear and rear the new generation, they have immense influence over the socialisation and education of children and this is particularly evident in the way in which children's aspirations are shaped, and is in turn reflected in the exceptional educational attainment of farm children.

The study then not only attempts to make farm women's subordination explicit, but in discerning the sources and force of their influence within and outside the farm family, offers a challenge to existing explanations of the evolution of Irish social structures on and off the farm.

The remaining chapters of the book contain an account of the research which was carried out in the west and east of Ireland. In the second chapter I review some of the theoretical issues involved in understanding women's involvement in family farming. In this I elaborate on the theoretical position outlined above which involves drawing on debates about the future of family farming, feminist theories of women's work and the sociology of the family, and argue that understanding women's situation involves seeing them as active agents involved in production, consumption and reproduction. In Chapter Three, I discuss the issues encountered in researching a topic of this nature and describe how the research was carried out. Chapter Four is about marriage and begins with an analysis of the way in which women's actions, whether avoiding marriage to farmers or becoming farm wives, affect the evolution of rural structures. I then go on to analyse some aspects of the marriage experiences of the women in the study. The work of farm wives is the focus of Chapter Five, including the work that they do on and off the farm and in the household; how they are constrained by the gendered organisation of work; and the way in which patriarchal power relations are contested and negotiated through the working relationship. Chapter Six is concerned with differential consumption and specifically with the distribution of resources within the farm family and how this is structured by gender. In Chapter Seven I have explored the ways in which women, through their role as mothers and their influence over education and socialisation, construct the future for their children. While farm women may not inherit the land, they nevertheless exert an immense influence on both the reproduction of family farming and the wider social order. In the final chapter, I discuss the main issues which emerge from the research and what I consider the implications of the findings for sociological theories of agrarian restructuring and feminist theories of the family.

2

WOMEN, FARM AND FAMILY IN IRELAND

Concepts and Issues

Introduction

Family farming is distinctive in that family members are engaged, simultaneously and in the same site, in producing goods for the market and for their own consumption. The usually clear-cut distinctions between production/consumption/reproduction, home and work are blurred. Clearly, gender relations lie at the very heart of the family farm business and are fundamental to the continuity of family farming as a social form. Indeed access to farming and the ownership of land and other assets are all structured on the basis of gender. Women work on family farms while they also bear and rear a new generation of farm children who are potential family farm labour. Yet much of the theorising about family farming in advanced capitalist societies has been based on unitary notions of the farm family where internal consensus is taken for granted and/or the coincidence of farm and family is ignored or considered irrelevant. The emphasis has been on the articulation of family farming with external capitals rather than on internal family relations. However, attempting to explore women's influence on the evolution of family farming involves looking inside the 'black box' of the farm family and requires a broadening of traditional theoretical horizons beyond the farm itself.

Feminist theories of the household and the family (the two are of course not necessarily synonymous, but they generally are in contemporary family farming in Ireland) have provided some important insights into intra-family processes. But here too, much of the focus has been on the relationship between capitalism and the family, particularly in attempts to theorise women's domestic labour. Farm families, as such, have been an object of study only in so far as they represent a particular case, where the family is the site of production as well as consumption. To develop a theoretical framework for understanding the farm family it is necessary to draw on two debates which have evolved quite separately from distinct 'problems' in sociology but which have some similar strands. The first of these concerns the family farm itself and how we can understand its survival/dissolution in advanced capitalist societies. The second centres around feminist accounts of the family as a social construct and as the locus of sets of social relations which are structured by gender. Apart from these wider sociological debates, we also need to explore what Irish rural sociology has revealed about the evolution of family farming and the farm family in Ireland. This chapter then is structured around these three bodies of work which provide the theoretical foundation for the present study.

Family Farming in Ireland

Sociological studies of agrarian social change in Ireland have been characterised by a number of significant features. Firstly – and almost certainly because Arensberg and Kimball's classic study of farming families in County Clare in the 1930s became a kind of benchmark – most studies of changes in family farming have been based on empirical data from the west of Ireland. The works of Scully (1971), Hannan (1972, 1979), Brody (1973), Scheper-Hughes (1979), Curtin (1986), Curtin and Varley (1987) and Kelleher and O'Hara (1978) are just some examples. Indeed a central contention of these studies has been that family farming in the west is distinctly different from the more commercialised farming areas in the east and south. The particular problems of the west have long been acknowledged at policy level and the region has been the target of special measures and programmes throughout this century.

Secondly, studies of agrarian change have, in the main, been concerned with the disintegration and restructuring of family farming rather than its persistence (see Commins et al., 1978; Kelleher and O'Mahony, 1984). Concepts such as decline, displacement, alienation, demoralisation, fatalism, and marginalisation have been central to these analyses. The decline in the number of smaller farms (though not holdings), demographic imbalances associated with migration from rural areas, the high incidence of bachelorhood among farmers (sometimes conceptualised as family failure), and the widening disparities in farm incomes have been explained largely in terms of the modernisation and commercialisation of agriculture and the regressive effects of state and EU support policies.

Thirdly, these concerns are associated with a major theoretical debate in Irish rural sociology which took place during the 1970s. This centred on the issue of the distinctiveness of the 'peasant system' among western smallholders which had earlier been characterised by Arensberg and Kimball. Gibbon (1973), in a trenchant critique of Arensberg and Kimball's functionalism and Brody's (1973) account of demoralisation and decline, dismissed the specificity of the west of Ireland case. Hannan (1979, 1982), on the other hand, has consistently argued that there existed a unique peasant system among western smallholders. Tovey (1992) has pointed out that what was really at issue here was the fate of family farming rather than the accuracy of the Arensberg and Kimball model. Gibbon (1973) contended that capitalist encroachment in agriculture leads inexorably to the dissolution of the peasantry so that demoralisation and decline are inevitable points on the road to extinction. Hannan (1979), on the other hand, argued that the western peasant system, with its own internal logic, was transformed rather than obliterated by incorporation into the capitalist world market. Tovey suggests that Hannan came closest to understanding contemporary family farming in Ireland by recognising that it is 'profoundly shaped by kinship and family factors'. In fact she argues that Hannan's analysis in his 1979 work *Displacement and Development* predated contemporary commoditisation theory by emphasising the importance of non-commoditised relationships in commercial family farming (1992: 100).

In the aftermath of Ireland's accession in 1973 to what is now the European Union, research on changes in farm structures shifted more towards a concentration on the dislocations associated with agricultural adjustment, and focused particularly on those farmers who were becoming marginalised, rather than on the survivors who were becoming commercial family farmers (see Kelleher and O'Hara 1978; Kelleher and O'Mahony, 1984; O'Hara, 1986). These studies drew attention to, inter alia, the heterogeneity within the farm population in terms of farm income and access to the means of production; the increasing reliance on non-farm income (particularly state transfers) among farm families; the role of the state and EU in the adjustment process; the need to see family farming as part of the wider agricultural economy in which commercial interests dominate; and the demographic adjustments associated with agricultural restructuring. This concern with the family farm and its economic viability throughout the 1980s overshadowed the emphases on family and kinship which had been evident in the earlier research referred to above.

Despite considerable restructuring, family farming in Ireland has not evolved in the way that some had anticipated, in so far as the decrease in the numbers of farmers (those who classify themselves occupationally as such) has not been accompanied by a commensurate consolidation of holdings and the emergence of a class of capitalist farmers. Breen et al., surveying the pattern of change in the numbers of farm holdings in Ireland from 1926 to 1981, concluded that 'although small farms are becoming less numerous it appears that for the most part, non-viable, marginal holdings can continue to exist from one generation to the next, often in the hands of owners whose primary occupation is not farming' (1990: 191). Despite the apparent incapacity of the majority of farm holdings to generate an adequate income (comparable to those obtaining outside farming), family farming persists as a social form. Hannan and Commins (1992) have suggested that pluriactivity has allowed landholders on small holdings to continue in farming, but it is not clear whether this increased reliance on non-farm income is part of the re-creation of new forms of family enterprise or simply a means of postponing the eventual demise of family farming. On the other hand, the commercial farm sector has undergone considerable change. The active involvement of these farms in the dynamics of agriculture as a business may make them analytically distinct from those more marginal to agricultural production. It may be that commercial farms are not only materially more prosperous but that family farming on such farms also involves a different and distinctive culture and farming logic.

Changes in Agriculture in Advanced Capitalist Societies

In contrast to much of the Irish sociological debate outlined above, a large part of which was influenced by modernisation theory, the predominant theoretical approach to understanding agrarian social change in advanced capitalist societies in recent decades has addressed the persistence of family farming rather than its decline. Derived from Marxist analysis, this political economy[1] approach to the study of agrarian social structures concentrates primarily on the way in which capitalism relates to rural economies and the links between capitalist expansion and agricultural restructuring. Much of the impetus for this approach derives from the realisation by neo-Marxists that the traditional Marxist assumptions about the evolution of agriculture have not been borne out

1. For a general review of the development of this approach see Buttel (1982), and for Britain, see Marsden et al. (1986a).

in practice in Western capitalist societies. According to classic Marxism, petty commodity producers in capitalist social formations are either 'anomalous relics of the pre-capitalist past' or 'disguised proletarians' or 'disguised capitalists' (Bernstein, 1986: 5). The empirical and theoretical inadequacies of this restrictive model of capitalist development have given rise to theoretical approaches which focus on either the relationships between petty commodity production and capitalism, or the resilience of simple commodity production. This 'resilience approach', in seeking to explain what is unique or distinctive about family farming, finds a parallel in attempts among feminist sociologists to theorise women's domestic labour, as we shall see later in this chapter.

Theorists have used different terminology when conceptualising the future of family farming – the terms 'family farmers', 'petty commodity producers', and 'simple commodity producers' are among the most commonly used. The term 'family farming' is itself easily amenable to conceptual confusion, so in this discussion, I use the term simple commodity production (SCP) to refer to a form of agricultural production characterised by the use of family labour, involving production mainly for the market, in which the means of production – land and capital – are in family ownership. Land is usually acquired and disposed of through kinship. Two main conceptualisations of the place of SCP in advanced capitalism can be discerned from the literature. The first of these posits SCP as being essentially outside of capitalism but under increasing pressure from its relentless forces. This is referred to as the process of subsumption. In one version of this approach SCP is under pressure and set to eventually disappear; in another, maintenance of SCP is seen as functional for capitalism which exploits it. What distinguishes both versions is their focus on the relationships between SCP and the wider economy. The second main conceptualisation of SCP focuses on its internal relations, particularly on the flexibility and adaptability of family labour processes within SCP which enable family farming to resist capitalist penetration. Both approaches come under the general rubric of commoditisation theory, in which commoditisation is seen as a historical process whereby exchange-value comes to assume an increasingly important role in economies, so that the measurement of value is achieved through the market (Long, 1986).

Capitalism and Family Farming

De Janvry (1980), following Marx (1976) and Lenin (1946), argued that the long-term forces of capitalism ensure that agricultural capital will eventually become concentrated in the hands of an agricultural bourgeoisie, while SCP will become marginalised, with farmers having to depend on off-farm work for a livelihood or having to abandon farming altogether. Other theorists have argued that SCP will persist only as long as certain conditions associated with primary agricultural production make it unattractive to capital. These conditions include seasonality, unpredictability, and excess of production over labour time. As long as technology is unable to overcome these difficulties, agriculture will be left to SCP (Mann and Dickinson, 1978; Mottura and Pugliese, 1980; Mann, 1990; Goodman and Redclift 1985, 1988). Goodman and Redclift have argued that:

> The capitalist development of agriculture can be conceptualised as the competitive movement of industrial capitalism to create sectors of valorisation by re-structuring the inherited 'pre-industrial' labour process. Industry has progressively appropriated activities related to production and processing which at earlier conjunctures were regarded as integral elements of the rural land-based production process.(1985: 232–33)

Thus capital has progressively moved in on SCP and agriculture has become more and more commoditised. The point made is that the subsumption process is relentless and that the family farm persists only because technology has not yet been able to overcome some of the limitations of land and nature. According to Goodman and Redclift, this process has been obscured by powerful ideologies of family farming which attribute its survival to its characteristics as a social form.

An alternative view is that the evolutionary path predicted by Marx has occurred only in exceptional cases, but that capitalism has succeeded in exploiting SCP by controlling the spheres of access and distribution (inputs and markets). The nature of primary production makes it convenient for capital to allow farming to remain as SCP. Nevertheless, by controlling the sphere of access and distribution, the capitalist mode of production reduces the farmer to the status of a proletarian who works at home (Amin and Vergopolous, 1974). Davis (1980) builds on and elaborates this thesis by arguing that the labour of the family farmer is exploited in much the same way as a piece-worker in industry, in that capital, by controlling the input and marketing sectors, exploits the labour of the primary producer whose 'independence' is a myth. It is in fact functional for capital to have the family farmer engaged in a production process which serves the interests of capital. These exploitative relations between corporate capital and SCP occur in their 'purest' form in contract farming, which is effectively the extraction of surplus value from the farm by capitalist firms who control the actual production process. Exploitation may also occur through farm indebtedness particularly when this involves surrendering transfers of value and entrepreneurial control (e.g., what crops to grow, stock to sell) to the lending agency. Farmers may also be exploited when purchasing inputs in monopolistic markets.

Each of these analyses, whether predicting the eventual annihilation of SCP as soon as technological development permits capital to take over primary production (in some sectors such as poultry production, technological advance has already allowed capitalist penetration), or arguing that SCP is incorporated into the capitalist mode of production but exploited by it, seem to have several shortcomings if we consider them in the light of the Irish case. In the first place they are inherently deterministic, in so far as the relentless logic of capitalist development does not allow for specific adaptations reflecting local or regional circumstances and historical events which create unique conditions. In Ireland's case, the distinctiveness of the land structure resulting from the abolition of the landlord system in the late nineteenth century had a crucial effect on the subsequent pattern of farming, the class structure of farming, and the ideological commitment to the 'family farm'. Secondly, the persistence of a majority of farm families who rely increasingly on off-farm income sources with no apparent commensurate trend towards either the concentration of land or the evolution of a capitalist class of farmers, suggests that unitary explanations of capitalist development might obscure rather than elucidate its complexities. Thirdly, these approaches take little account of state intervention in agriculture, despite its obvious significance. State action in Ireland both pre- and post-EU accession has had the effect of increasing incomes from farming through price support, and stimulating investment through the provision of capital grants, and as I have argued elsewhere (O'Hara, 1986), the net effect of state policy in Ireland has been to accentuate existing income disparities within the farm population. Nevertheless, EU transfers, such as compensatory payments to livestock farmers in Less Favoured Areas, have become essential components of farm income in such areas.

Finally, and most important for the present study, farm families are not included in these analyses which are overly structuralist and make little allowance for human agency. They cannot therefore address the possibility of differing interests within the farm family, particularly the fact that farm labour flexibility may be predicated on the exploitation of women's labour. The responses of individual households to the changing opportunities in the world around them (in the labour market for instance) can not easily be accommodated, yet empirical diversity suggests many possible forms of accommodation with external capitals. More recent applications of the commoditisation approach have attempted to address some of these issues. However before turning to these, it is necessary to look at the alternative theoretical position mentioned above – the idea that it is the internal characteristics of SCP as a specific 'form' of production which allow it to survive in the face of increased encroachment from capitalism.

SCP as a Form of Production – Friedmann's Approach

One of the most prominent contributors to the debate on the future of family farming is Friedmann (1978, 1980, 1981). Friedmann's point of departure is that SCP is a form of production (as distinct from a mode of production, such as capitalism) within capitalism. SCP, she argues, is characterised by commoditisation – the enterprise sells its product and purchases what it requires for consumption – therefore it must exist within a capitalist regime of factor markets for land, labour and credit. What distinguishes SCP from capitalism are the relations of production at the enterprise level. The constant re-creation of its characteristic social relations, Friedmann refers to as 'reproduction'. This involves mechanisms for the renewal of raw materials and tools through productive consumption, and of labour through personal consumption.

While the internal relations of capitalism are determined by value, those of SCP involve other relations such as the gender division of labour and kinship. What is crucial is that SCP, by combining ownership and labour in a set of social relations in which there is no structural requirement for surplus profit, is uniquely different from capitalism. Friedmann argues that in certain conditions SCP has advantages over capitalism as a form of production specifically because of its internal relations. Profit is not a condition of reproduction and personal consumption can be adjusted, unlike wages, when production conditions are unfavourable. On the one hand, when family labour is scarce workers can be hired. On the other, the requirements for reproduction can be met, if necessary, through individual family members engaging in off-farm employment. Despite economies of scale associated with capitalism, the nature of the agricultural enterprise (in which SCP is so prevalent) and even the technological innovations associated with agriculture may favour SCP – hence its persistence.

SCP then, shares with peasant production the unity of family and property. The idea that SCP as a form of production is superior to capitalism because of its flexibility and adaptability (farm families can reduce their consumption when returns from farming are low) is similar to the concept of 'self exploitation' which has its roots in classic materialist analysis and the work of Kautsky (Banaji, 1980) and Chayanov

(1925). Bernstein's (1977) concept of the 'simple reproduction squeeze' which often involves reduced levels of consumption and indebtedness and the run down of land in agriculture is also similar. The fate of SCP in the final analysis rests on its capacity to maintain its competitive advantages and the persistence of internal structures which provide the basis for flexibility. This idea of explaining the resilience of SCP as intrinsic to its features as a social form is not greatly dissimilar to Hannan's (1979) account of the durability of the peasant system in the west of Ireland to which we have referred already. Both recognise the importance of family processes in ensuring the continuance of this form of production, although Hannan's theoretical position would differ considerably from that of Marxist political economy.

In a later article, Friedmann (1986b) has argued that there is nothing specific to agriculture which accounts for the persistence of forms of production such as SCP. Rather, to understand SCP in capitalist economies we must look at its distinct characteristics as a form. These are the ownership of property and the organisation of labour through kinship, gender and age. Unequal relations within the enterprise are associated with age and gender and are often reinforced by property rights. It is the interplay of household and business that gives family enterprises their essential dynamic. In this context she draws attention to the importance of succession in farm families and the influence of internal relations such as conflicting expectations by spouses or children, and external relations such as prices and markets, on family processes. The family enterprise is subject to pressures both as a family and as an enterprise (1986b: 46). Women's involvement as managers of the domestic domain is critical to the resolution of tension between investment and consumption goals. Farm women are frequently and simultaneously household managers, conflict mediators and farm workers. More fundamentally, gender roles are institutionalised in the legal code, so that farm wives may not have legal rights commensurate with their de facto involvement. According to Friedmann, the contradiction between women's equality and the ideology of family farming rarely becomes explicit (1986b: 55).

In Ireland a recent example of this tension between ideology and women's status was the fear, widely expressed during the debate on divorce,[2] of the fragmentation of farm holdings which might result from the introduction of divorce legislation. Farm wives' legal entitlement to land or family assets in the event of divorce, which would be integral to such legislation, was seen as potentially threatening to the

---

2. There was no legal provision for divorce in Ireland until 1996. Introduction of divorce legislation necessitated a referendum, which was held in 1995, to change the constitution. The decision to remove the ban on divorce was carried by a small majority.

stability of family farming in Ireland. A further example is the documented reservation of the representative of the Irish Farmers Association to one of the recommendations on community property in the Second Commission on the Status of Women. Recommendation 1.5.6(c) advocated the immediate introduction of a regime of community property in marriage, providing for a legal share of one half of the estate where the other spouse dies testate (i.e., having made a will). The reservation reads:

> While in general terms equal share rights are certainly desirable, in cases such as family farms maintaining the viability of farm holdings must also be considered and the need for equity between parents and family members. In this regard, while a 50:50 split may be reasonable in families of one or two children, where there are more than two children it might be more practicable to maintain the one-third legal share provided in the Succession Act, 1965. (Second Commission on the Status of Women, 1993: 58)

The significance of Friedmann's work is that she has drawn attention to the importance of ideology in family farming and, in attempting to understand the persistence of family farming in advanced capitalist societies, she shifts the emphasis towards SCP as a social form, in which the internal dynamics are as important as the structure, i.e., it is as important to understand the farm family as it is to understand the farm business. Family farming is not simply an economic system being buffeted by the forces of capitalism, but the site of complex social relations in which gender is a central dynamic.

Commoditisation and Human Agency

Commoditisation theory, as an attempt to understand the fate of family farming in capitalist societies, has been concerned with two central themes – the relationships between SCP and the wider capitalist economy and the social processes internal to SCP itself (Whatmore, 1991). Both the approaches outlined above have been criticised and there have been some recent attempts at a synthesis. The critique centres on the fact that macro-structural theories of capitalism give little theoretical space to the actions of individuals, i.e., human agency. Commoditisation theory is said to encapsulate a linear view of agrarian development which is excessively structuralist and economistic and fails to theorise differential responses to change. In such a conceptualisation human actors do not figure or are seen as hapless victims of structural processes. Moreover, the significance of culture and ideology has received little attention from commoditisation theorists (Long, 1986; Whatmore, 1991). As Long et al., in their introduction to *The Commoditisation Debate* point out:

> It is necessary to bring farmers and simple commodity producers back into the picture in order to explore what commoditisation means in the everyday life of those it affects. Adopting such an actor oriented perspective directs one towards the study of diversity and variation in social process, which, in this case, highlights such critical aspects as farmer and/or household strategy, and the management of the labour process. (1986: 6)

Vandergeest (1988) has stressed the importance of what he calls 'extra-economic' coercion (such as that found in the patriarchal family) in structuring the lives of farmers, and the need to understand how transformations in the cultural and political, as well as economic, spheres affect agrarian structures. His critique ends with the simple, but nevertheless appropriate, plea for theorists to 'take seriously what people say' (1988: 26), a feature notably missing from much of the commoditisation literature.

In attempting to confront some of these criticisms van der Ploeg (1986, 1990) has distinguished two forms of reproduction in commoditised agriculture which he terms autonomous and market dependent and which can then be linked with farmer strategies. Van der Ploeg argues that the apparent diversity in present-day European agriculture can be best explained as involving different 'farming styles' which reflect different ways of organising farm labour. Farmers will respond to market forces and technology with different logic which will in turn be influenced by their cultural heritage. Within the constraints of the market, technological development and agricultural and rural policy, farmers have found 'room to manoeuvre', to impose their own 'style' on SCP (1993: 249–50).[3]

Van der Ploeg has succeeded in bringing simple commodity producers back into the picture as active agents. However, in equating farming styles and strategies wholly with the actions of individual farmers, he does this in a way that is gender and family blind and which is reminiscent of the adoption/diffusion studies of the 1960s. When he acknowledges intra-family processes at all, it is to suggest that the farm wives are becoming less influential and more subordinated by the requirements of the farm enterprise (1993: 246–47). If this is the case, then it surely has implications for family farming. It may mean that women are withdrawing to the household, or that they are distancing themselves from

3. This approach had earlier been used in a study of west of Ireland farming by one of van der Ploeg's students. See Leeuwis (1997).

the family farm, thereby changing the gendered structure of the farm labour process. In equating the future of farming with the 'logic' of the male farmer, van der Ploeg avoids these issues and suggests that the goal-orientated and multifaceted behaviour of farmers should be the starting point for agrarian scientific research.

Friedmann's theorising has stimulated a debate about SCP as a concept (see Goodman and Redclift, 1985; Friedmann, 1986a; and Whatmore et al., 1986). The main point of contention is whether SCP is a stage in the process of subsumption or a uniquely different 'form of production' as Friedmann argues. Whatmore et al. (1986) accuse Friedmann of being preoccupied with form (especially in her emphasis on the presence or absence of wage labour) to the extent of precluding her from examining process, and particularly the analysis of unique sets of internal relations and the relationship between SCP and external capitals. To demonstrate this they have developed a fourfold 'relational typology' of farm businesses in England which reflects the interaction between the subsumption process and the specific circumstances of individual farms, that is, the degree to which they are directly or indirectly commoditised (Whatmore et al., 1987a, 1987b). Direct commoditisation is a variable process which, at its extreme, involves the transformation to corporate ownership of land and capital, hired labour and management; indirect commoditisation involves varying degrees of capitalist control of inputs, markets, credit and technology. However, this typology does not address the farm family as a social form or the way in which different family members relate to the wider structural processes associated with the process of subsumption, a point which Whatmore et al. acknowledge (1987b: 120–21).

Marsden et al. have further extended this typology by attempting to 'incorporate aspects of the social reproduction of farm families into the analysis of subsumption directly' (1992: 409). Drawing on empirical data from Britain, they focus on the relationship between capital's need to accumulate and farm families' desire to maintain control inter-generationally. Marsden et al. construct a set of social trajectories of family farms based on the farmer's expectations of succession and the origins of the farm. Their analysis reveals that family dynamics and market mechanisms can be mutually reinforcing. Farm families effectively use commoditised relations for social ends. Family farming is important to families in England and is not in danger of being subsumed by capital after all. In fact family farming is under greatest pressure on the least subsumed farms. Marsden and his colleagues have therefore suggested that lack of capitalist penetration, rather than the reverse, may represent the most serious threat to the family farms they studied. They can only explain this reversal of conventional analyses of SCP by suggesting a strong commitment to continuity/succession among farm families (1992: 424–25). However, as the authors admit, the limitations of their data cannot reveal the intra-family dynamics by which the desire for continuity and its achievement through succession is negotiated or how it is structured by gender relations. The discovery and elaboration of some of these dynamics was clearly a major objective of the present research.

Apart from the work of Whatmore (1991) which will be discussed below, commoditisation theory, while frequently acknowledging the importance of gender and intra-family processes, has in practice remained largely gender-blind in seeking to deal with the question of agency. Although the family is clearly implicated in, for instance, the commitment to continuity suggested by Marsden et al. (1992), the empirical focus on the farm operator precludes any possibility of revealing the family processes which underlie it. Similarly while van der Ploeg (1993) acknowledges the existence of women on family farms, he then proceeds to treat them as if they are irrelevant and without influence.

Before turning more specifically to reviewing the literature on women on family farms, it is worth noting briefly that other theorists, outside the political economy tradition, have dealt with the agency/structure problem by using the concept of 'survival strategies' to capture the complexity of ways in which farm families adapt to the forces of commoditisation. What actually constitutes survival in this situation is not always clear, but the term 'survival strategy' has been used widely to describe any set of actions initiated by farm household members to ensure continuity on the farm holding. The concept of survival strategies may avoid the determinism inherent in more structuralist explanations of the evolution of family farming, but by not allowing for the existence of unequal relations or different interests within it, a unitary idea of the farm family is implied (Redclift, 1986; Crow, 1989). Similar criticisms have been made of the concept of 'household strategies' pioneered by Gershuny (1983) and Pahl as 'the best use of resources for 'getting by' under given social and economic conditions' (Pahl, 1984:20). Such a conceptualisation does not allow space to theorise gender inequality (Walby, 1990) and, in addition to its unitary connotations, the notion of household strategy implies voluntarism which distracts from constraints such as the labour market and cultural and ideological influences embodied in local social practice (Morris, 1990). Even when the idea of patriarchal control is incorporated into the 'survival strategy' concept, it can merely replace one determinism with another by substituting the 'natural' division of labour with 'patriarchal control' as 'natural', leaving the social processes involved largely unexplored (see Pile, 1991). The concept of survival strategies does not allow us to capture what happens inside the family and whether the actions of women and men differentially affect outcomes (Redclift and Whatmore, 1990).

Women and Family Farming

Friedmann (1981, 1986a, 1986b), as has been noted above, emphasised that it is the conjunction of farm and family that is the unique feature of family farming. More importantly she pointed to the significance of the family as a locus for conflicting interests and unequal power relations. Yet, subsequent attempts to deal with the problem of agency in commoditisation theory have largely ignored her insights and (with the exception of Whatmore, 1991) fail to theorise the farm family. Commoditisation theory has serious shortcomings in providing a complete understanding of the evolution of family farming.

When we turn to studies of women's involvement in family farming we find some equally significant limitations. Such studies have, in the main, focused rather narrowly on women's work for the family farm as an enterprise, largely ignoring their work in the household or off the farm and failing to consider at all their involvement in consumption or reproduction. Fassinger and Schwarzweller (1984) have suggested that many of these studies have serious shortcomings both methodologically and conceptually. Many are based on investigations of small unrepresentative samples or populations usually of white (in the U.S.) farmers' wives. There is often no clear rationale for the farm tasks selected to quantify women's involvement (see especially Jones and Rosenfeld's [1981] national sample in the U.S., and Buchanan et al., 1982, in Britain). Even the factors associated with various levels of involvement are frequently not investigated. The nature of the farm enterprise, stage in the family life-cycle, women's previous experiences in the labour force, their training and their own perceptions of their roles are frequently overlooked. Some studies rely solely on the male farm operator's account of his spouse's work.

Theoretically, many of these studies are part of a tradition in rural sociology which is heavily influenced by modernisation theory. The importance of the family as a 'unit of production' in agriculture is acknowledged, but it is then left aside as if it was a haven of social order and 'unity/equity' separate from the economy, while the farm becomes the unit of analysis. Women's work in the household and its links to the reproduction of the family farm enterprise are ignored, as is the complexity of family and kin relations in which family farming is embedded. Access to farming is determined by kinship, and in a patrimonial system women rarely inherit farms; they enter farming mainly through marriage. In this way they find themselves in the midst of a kin group associated with a form of production over which they have little direct control. Few women are sole owners of farm enterprises (until they are widowed) and this situation has changed little in recent times (see Geisler et al., 1985). To understand women's involvement in family farming therefore, it is not sufficient to focus on their role in farm production, we must also look to the totality of their involvement in the family farm, in production, consumption and reproduction.

Although farm women as such have rarely been the specific objects of study in Ireland, we do know quite a lot about them because of the research attention given in Irish rural sociology to the farm family. Arensberg and Kimball provided a detailed account of the gender divisions in farm families on smallholdings in the west of Ireland in the 1930s and this is fully discussed in Chapter Five in the context of an analysis of the work of farm women. Subsequent, mainly anthropological, studies (McNabb, 1964; Messenger, 1969; Brody, 1973; Scheper Hughes, 1979; Hannan and Katsiaouni, 1977) have also provided important insights into intra-family processes in farm families. These studies have been criticised by Shortall (1991) for failing to adopt a gender perspective or question a social order in which women were clearly subordinate. This seems a somewhat unrealistic demand, given the pre-feminist era when many of these studies were carried out. However, Shortall misses the opportunity to articulate what they do tell us about women in Irish farm families and to question the processes which lead to the continued eclipse of gender as an issue in Irish rural sociology (Tovey, 1992).

The transformation of the Irish agricultural economy in the post-war period was, as has already been mentioned, characterised by commercialisation of farm production involving mechanisation and specialisation and widening income disparities between large and small holdings and between the east and west regions. These changes had a major impact on the labour process on family farms, particularly the work of women. Commercialisation and specialisation meant that traditional farmyard activities such as pig and poultry production became highly commercialised on a small number of specialist farms. The specialisation and decline in tillage, and the shift from hay to silage as winter fodder reduced the manual labour involved in fieldwork. New technology (such as milking machines/milking parlours, refrigerated milk-cooling) altered the nature of the labour requirements on dairy farms. There was also a gradual improvement in living standards associated with rural electrification and the installation of piped water, followed in recent decades by the construction of many new homes. While these improvements reduced the physical labour required of farm women they also coincided with higher standards of domestic management which resulted in women spending more time on actual housework. Studies of the introduction of domestic labour-saving devices in other countries have shown that their potential to reduce women's domestic work is offset by the demands of rising standards (Vanek, 1980; Cowan, 1983).

The kinds of changes in family farming just described were bound to affect social relations inside the farm family. In their study of farm families in the west of Ireland, Hannan and Katsiaouni (1977) set out to investigate alterations in farm family interaction since Arensberg and Kimball documented them in the 1930s, and the factors associated with these changes. At the beginning of the study they argue that changes in farm production and family consumption patterns have weakened the role of the farm wife in farm production, forcing her to withdraw to the household (1977: 24–26). However, this seems somewhat at odds with the findings of their empirical analysis which revealed that, on more than half the farms studied, farm wives' contribution to the farm production process was highly significant (1977: 71). On two-thirds of all the farms the contribution of wives and younger children was regarded as extremely important by husbands, to the point that without such help, some lines of production would have to be dropped. Despite this fact, and their observation that wives in farm families tended to play a central role in the financial management of farms, Hannan and Katsiaouni concluded that the end point of change in women's roles is towards the 'wifehood', 'motherhood' and even 'housewifely' role models of the urban middle class (1977: 188). How they arrive at this conclusion is somewhat puzzling, given their empirical data and the fact that they admit that they did not gather information about wives' own views on their participation in farm work.

Their conclusion that women are withdrawing to the home is based on an analysis of role expectations of spouses, the affectional bonds between them, and the stage in the family life-cycle, rather than their actual work roles. This leads them to conflate changes in the ideology of marriage and the nature of the marital relationship with changes in farm women's work roles. Their extensive use of Likert and Guttman scales to measure the various dimensions of marriage relationships, while demonstrating their complexity, obscures women's work roles. For instance, husbands' rather than wives' responses were used in the measurement of wives' participation in farm tasks and, even then, only a very narrow range of manual tasks were included (1977: 44,102). Moreover, although their analysis examines in great detail the task and decision-making roles of husbands and wives, it does so in a way that is curiously gender-blind in taking for granted the conventional distinctions between home and farm and in leaving unchallenged the patriarchal structures which maintain male dominance on the farm and female dominance in the home. For instance, they find it surprising that 'such a large proportion of wives play such an active role in what are culturally defined as basically male domains' (1977: 71). They also found that farm women generally preferred farm work to the dreariness of housework and would like to do more farm work if they had the time. This leads them to suggest that Arensberg and Kimball were wrong in suggesting that women found 'reward and pleasure' in their very segregated work roles. However, they fail to question the significance of the gendered division of labour for either the couple themselves or the farm family, or why the gendered cultural prescriptions should be so strong. While they recognise the different statuses attached to gender roles, the origin and persistence of these is unquestioned (Shortall, 1991: 324).

Hannan and Katsiaouni's work is important not only for its insights and in its uniqueness as the only study of interaction in Irish farm families but also in that it raises a number of issues which are relevant for the present discussion. Firstly, they drew attention to the fact that farm women were dissatisfied with their roles and to the relationship between this dissatisfaction and changing ideologies of marriage in favour of more egalitarian relationships. Secondly, they pointed out the significance of husbands' power (or wives' powerlessness) over the pattern of family interaction. Associated with this is the fact that, although the familial role expectations of farm wives had changed, the behaviour of their husbands in a large proportion of cases had not (1977: 184). Thirdly, their assertion that the quality of the affectional relationship between spouses is a crucial variable in explaining task roles implies that we examine not just what women do, but the relationship within which they do it, and their understanding of the significance of their work for the family farm. In this sense their work foreshadowed later feminist concepts such as Whitehead's (1981) idea of the 'conjugal contract'. Finally, their assertion that family roles are nowadays negotiated rather than culturally prescribed, and that clashing role expectations between spouses result in a high degree of dissatisfaction among farm wives, hints at a degree of resistance and agency among farm women sometimes absent from more contemporary feminist studies. It also suggests that we should look at how farm women today seek to resolve this conflict and how they resist culturally prescribed roles.

Feminism and Family Labour

Feminist theory takes as its starting point inequalities in gender relations, and the idea of gender itself as a social construct which orders human interactions. It has had a major impact on social theory, particularly by opening to scrutiny areas of social life previously consigned to the private and personal. Central to feminist theorising is the concept of patriarchy as male domination over women, so that gender relations are fundamentally relations of power. One of the most visible manifestations of patriarchy is in the control and appropriation of women's labour, and early feminist theorists such as Firestone (1970) and Mitchell (1971) were among the first to consider the links between the subordination of women and their work in the family and confinement to the domestic sphere. Much of the subsequent development of feminist theory has involved an attempt to construct a materialist theory of women's subordination. In practical terms this has meant that feminists have examined women's work – what it is, what they get paid for, and how conceptions of women's work change historically and are reinforced by ideology (Eisenstein, 1985). A significant area of discussion has been that of domestic labour – what women do in the household and how their work can be characterised and interpreted. In recent decades these debates have broadened to an analysis of the family – bringing about a decisive shift away from the Parsonian functionalist interpretation, prominent in the 1950s and 1960s (Cheal, 1991). This work, at both empirical and theoretical levels, has focused on the structured gender inequalities associated with separation of family and economy, the links between household structures and institutionalised power relations in the wider society, the family as a site of consumption, and the pervasiveness of the ideology of familism (Close, 1985; Collins, 1985; Barrett and McIntosh, 1982). A second body of literature has concentrated on household production in 'developing societies' showing deep-seated inequalities within households and how economic change impacts differently on women and men in these situations (Redclift and Mignione, 1985; Redclift and Whatmore, 1990).

The domestic labour debate (DLD), which dominated feminist theorising of women's work in the 1970s, has some interesting parallels with the political economy perspective on family farming, since both were attempting to explain what appear to be pre-capitalist anachronisms – family farming and unpaid domestic work – in order to understand their relationship to capitalism. In agrarian political economy, the primary structural separation is seen as between SCP and capitalist farming, while in the DLD it came to be perceived as a separation between the public and private spheres. The critical issue was how women's unpaid domestic labour was to be understood and specified. One strand of the debate (Bensten, 1969; Harrison, 1974) perceived the work of women in households as involving the creation of use values rather than commodities for the market. The household is conceptualised as an individual production unit – a 'pre-industrial' entity. Women's work, while socially necessary, is outside the capitalist economy. The production of use values is an integral part of capitalism, although the links between the use values of household production and its exchange values are not always immediately apparent. The use values of the housewife become exchange values when the labour-power produced and reproduced within the household is sold. The 'presumption of familial affection' obscures this economic relation.

Other theorists, notably Dalla Costa (1972) and Seccombe (1974) argued that women's labour only appears to be outside the capitalist economy, but is in fact an essential function in the production of surplus value. Gardiner (1976) suggested that domestic labour, by reproducing labour cheaply, contributes to capitalist profits, while Fox (1980) argued that were workers not supported by unpaid domestic labour, their wages would have to be much higher. Bennholdt-Thomsen (1981) grouped housewives and peasant producers together as the main subsistence producers in the capitalist world economy. She argued that both are integrated into capitalism through their marginalisation in that 'they form the consolidated mass of the industrial reserve army of labour and as such they are continuously reproduced as part of the extended reproduction of capital' (1981: 41). Long (1984) criticised Bennholdt-Thomsen's attempt to extend Marx's labour theory of value to domestic work, arguing that it is analytically impossible to demonstrate precisely how nonpaid domestic labour is subjected to the capitalist valorisation process. Furthermore, he argues, that concentration of the analysis on the way in which non-wage labour is subsumed by capital deflects attention from the nature of the actual social forms associated with different types of production and reproduction. As Walby (1990) concluded, Marxist feminist analysis overstates the links between women's labour and capitalism at the expense of gender equality itself. Finch (1983) similarly rejected functionalist 'serves the needs of capitalism' approaches, for their determinism which leaves no room for individuals to be social actors shaping and interpreting their own lives, and glosses over the differences between families in their domestic arrangements.

We have here then the same two problems already associated with the critique of commoditisation theory – the inability to comprehend empirical diversity and the problem of 'agency'. Moreover, Barrett (1980) and

Barrett and Mackintosh (1982) assert that the ideology of familism is at least as important in sustaining the family as its economic significance for capitalism, arguing that 'this institution is the focal point of a set of ideologies that resonate throughout society. The imagery of family life permeates the fabric of social existence and provides a highly significant, dominant and unifying complex of social meaning' (1982: 29). Capitalism and ideology conspire to keep women subordinate – firstly through women's material dependence on men and secondly through ideologies which reinforce and naturalise women's domestic role. We have already referred to the pervasiveness of family farm ideology in Ireland (Chapter One). How ideology is constructed, shaped and incorporated in, for instance, the legal code, its relation to material conditions, and the way in which changing ideologies affect women's lives are therefore important issues for empirical investigation when seeking to understand women's predicament in family farming.

Among the criticisms levelled at the DLD is the fact that wives of working-class men were the main empirical referents (Delphy and Leonard, 1992). Delphy (1984) is one of the few feminist theorists to look at women's work in small family businesses, where as she puts it 'the unit of production is the family'. In one of the most significant attempts to synthesise radical feminism (in which patriarchy, viewed as men's domination of women, is central) and materialist analyses, she rejects the view that it is the nature of women's work which explains their relationship to production. The obverse is the case according to Delphy – it is the relations of production in which women work (the patriarchal household) which explain why their work is excluded from the realm of value. Using French peasant households as an illustration, Delphy points out the significance of women's contribution to production for the market. This work, which is unpaid, cannot be separated from other work done by women such as child-rearing or housekeeping which are also unpaid. This labour is taken for granted in a system such as the family farm, where the family is the unit of production. The relationship between those who work on the farm unpaid and that of the farmer/father figure is one of exploitation. This subordination of women is carried over into official statistics where unpaid family labour is generally described as 'family help'. Following from this, Delphy argues that there can be no real distinction between use value and exchange value. That which has a use value and is consumed by the family could have been sold on the market – even the domestic work of women. The ultimate goal of the farm family is consumption and this is mediated by exchange, not that some activities are inherently productive and some are not. When it occurs within the family, women's work is regarded as 'unproductive' (and hence not included in GNP statistics). All women's work within the family is unpaid regardless of its ultimate outcome. It is in the family mode of production that what Delphy calls patriarchal exploitation occurs. Delphy sees the family mode of production as being distinctly different from capitalism and essentially outside of it because the relations of production within the household are different in character from the wage labour relations of capitalism. Although she has been criticised for her rather perfunctory analysis of capitalist relations (see Walby, 1990: 74), Delphy, along with Hartmann (1979) and Brown (1981) argues that capitalism and patriarchy are two distinct, if interrelated systems. The significance of Delphy's work is that she is one of the few radical feminists to look at the farm family as a mode of production. More importantly she has conceptualised women's labour differently and has attributed exploitation not to what women do but to the relations of production in which they work and the fact that their work is unpaid.

Domestic Political Economy – Whatmore's Feminist Reconstruction of Commoditisation

Whatmore's (1991) rigorous attempt to penetrate the black box of the family farm through a 'feminist reconstruction' of Marxist political economy is undoubtedly the most sophisticated attempt within this approach to theorise family farming. Whatmore argues that conventional political economy cannot accommodate a theory of the internal structure of the farm household, arguing that 'a theoretical framework is required which "problematises" the concepts of production and labour employed in analysing the family labour process and which "deconstructs" the family household in order to analyse the principal social division structuring its productive and reproductive relations – gender' (1991: 33–34).

She puts forward a theory of domestic political economy which incorporates patriarchal gender relations into the commoditisation model, arguing that the gender regime of the family can be seen as 'an integral part of a wider system of patriarchal gender relations' (1991: 37). Patriarchal gender relations operate at the micro level of the family farm through the labour process, marriage and kinship ties, economic dependence and ideologies of marriage. Central to Whatmore's theorising is her composite model of reproduction, encompassing production for both subsistence and the market, so that production and reproduction are seen as interlocking, rather than separate, processes. This, she argues, allows the family to be theorised as a social institution structured by gender and class relations instead of being hived off into the sphere of 'reproduction'. The concept of 'domestic political economy' is intended to capture what Whatmore calls the unity of production and reproduction. The components of an analysis of the family farm using this framework include the household structure, the labour process, ownership of capital and land, and linkages with external capitals.

Whatmore's concern with specifying the reproductive sphere and seeing the family as a site of both production and reproduction has its roots in long-standing ambiguities about the concept of reproduction and its various uses in sociology and agrarian studies. It has already been pointed out that most studies of women's involvement in agriculture in Europe and North America have concentrated on the 'productive sphere'. This has not been the case in the 'developing world' where anthropological studies of the household (Boserup, 1970; Goody, 1976; Meillassoux, 1981) have demonstrated the links between women's work and status, forms of marriage and inheritance, and the economic relations of production (Moore, 1988). In European rural sociology, however, consideration of women's involvement in reproduction and the links between reproduction and the wider processes of changes in agrarian formations remain largely unexplored. Yet the concept of reproduction is central both to understanding family farming and women's work in the household. It has however, been bedevilled by its usage alongside production as a kind of residual category, described by Walby (1990) as 'hopelessly flawed', since all the tasks typically designated as reproductive (food provision, childcare, cleaning, sexual and emotional services) are also commoditised and conventionally designated as 'production'. Delphy and Leonard conclude that the term 'reproduction' 'is used in a thoroughly sloppy way, and, at the limit, is merely another way of distinguishing women's (supposedly caring) work from men's (supposedly instrumental) work; and/or the rest of society from the capitalist mode of production' (1992: 63). Whatmore's solution to dualistic conceptualisations of production/reproduction is to theorise them as a unity, rather than as separate spheres (1991: 39). While this allows her to see all labour (not just the work of women) as 'reproductive' and to theorise the links between reproduction and production, she remains narrowly focused on the labour process and does not address the possibility of women's unique influence on reproduction. This is a point to which we return below.

In her empirical examination of family farming in Britain, Whatmore shows how patriarchal gender relations intersect with the commoditisation process through the organisation of family work and capital. Her survey of farm wives reveals their limited legal and financial interest in the farm, their restricted involvement in decision-making, and their lack of control over profits. Case study material from six family farms reveals how the labour process is a major instrument of subordination of women and how this is reinforced by ideology. The farm family is suffused with ideologies of 'wifehood' which legitimise patriarchal labour relations:

> The analysis shows how women themselves represent their work in ways which undervalue it or discount whole aspects of it as somehow not 'proper' work. . . However the implication is not that women are somehow 'duped' into acquiescing in their own subordination but that the relationship between the ideas and meanings constructed through subjective interpretation of the labour process, and the ways in which these ideas and meanings inform labour practices themselves is considerably more complex than notions of 'bias' or 'false consciousness' allow. (1991: 102)

Women's involvement in the labour process on and off the farm and the ideologies which underpin it are structured by the commoditisation process, so that what women actually do on the farm varies greatly. This is shown by the differences between 'farming women' who retain a significant involvement in the farm production process and 'incorporated wives' (no different from the wives of any business person). In the latter case, according to Whatmore (1991), the commoditisation process has fractured the link between production and reproduction, so that women have become marginal to the farm production process but are still tied to it by family capital and patrilineal kinship relations. The relationship between commoditisation, patriarchy and gender ideologies is not however, as Whatmore admits, 'neatly synchronised' but varies in specific historical and cultural contexts.

Whatmore's careful theorising clearly demonstrates the necessity of incorporating a theory of patriarchal gender relations into political economy theories about family farming. Although her theoretical position allows for the examination of other dimensions of power relations, farm women themselves emerge from the empirical analysis as having relatively little room for manoeuvre. It is difficult to discern any significant actions on their part which denote resistance to the patriarchal structures by which they are circumscribed or which can affect the evolution of the family enterprise. Concentration on the labour process precludes consideration of other aspects of the relationship between women's actions and the reproduction of family farming. These include how gender relations structure consumption and succession and particularly the significance of the mother role, as opposed to that of wife, and how it impacts on reproduction. In the end it is not clear whether women have (or can have) any effect on the evolution of family farming. Although Whatmore does refer to the 'structural tensions' within the gender relations of the family farm as being potentially transformative (1991: 144), she sees the limited collective action of farm women as being the only evidence that they are taking action because they are dissatisfied with their lot.

Women's Exploitation in the Family

Whatmore's attempt to reconstruct the political economy of family farming from a feminist perspective represents a major advance on previous theorising in a field dominated by indifference to gender. It is one of two recent works which have shaped and influenced the present study. The second of these is Delphy and Leonard's (1992) study in which they put forward a refined and expanded analysis of the family which extends earlier work by Delphy (1984). Delphy and Leonard regard the family as the locus of women's exploitation, arguing that 'families need to be analysed as socio-economic institutions; as structured hierarchical systems of social relations around the production, consumption and transmission of property' (1992: 2). Studies of the family (or households) ignore their internal structures, assuming that 'everyone is equal and everyone does the same sorts of things and gets the same share of resources' (1992: 19). By not seeing the family as economic in character sociologists have obscured its material nature.

Delphy and Leonard see patriarchy and capitalism as two distinct social systems which influence and structure each other. In this, their approach is similar to that of Hartmann (1979). The domestic labour debate, they argue, did not address gender relations directly, because the actual work done by women, the conditions in which they do it, and their feelings about it were not considered. The focus was rather on the connection between women's work and male wages or the function of their labour for capitalism (1992: 56). They also point out that while there is now widespread acceptance of the material basis of patriarchy, most feminist work has focused on the labour market rather than women's work in the family. Also, by concluding that there has been a move from 'private' to 'public' patriarchy (see Walby, 1990), because of women's increased involvement in the paid labour force, in public life generally, and because of the availability of divorce, feminist theory has turned away from the family as the principal site of women's subordination. A feminist analysis, they assert, 'must stop and focus on the relations of production of women themselves – and not be always upstream or downstream of them' (1992: 57)

The core of Delphy and Leonard's theoretical case rests on the position of the woman (wife or cohabitee) within the household as a dependent of the head. She does not own what she produces and is exploited so that 'wives' labour power is appropriated, for even when women have full-time paid employment they still do the bulk of childcare and domestic work'(1992: 117). Women are exploited in the family, not because of the work they do, but because of the relations of production in which they work (family-based households) and the fact that their work is unpaid. The definition of work in this context is quite specific. It is unpaid work done for the head of household within family household units. The concept of 'head of household' (HOH) is central to their analysis:

> Most households have one head, properly and usually a man, and he maintains its members. His dependants work for the general good of the group under his (hopefully benevolent) direction, and owe him love, respect, obedience – and various kinds of labour. (1992: 98)

They go on to say (1992: 112) that the head of the household always has control over the resources of the family, particularly market transactions. Wives therefore are subordinated by having to work unpaid for the HOH and all the material aspects of their lives are controlled by him. Women's and men's work is done in structurally different situations because he is working to support his dependants, whereas she is working for him. This, they say, applies even to women who have a separate personal income because they still do unpaid work (housework).

Indeed, capitalism and patriarchy may compete for women's labour and Delphy and Leonard (1992: 120) wonder whether the point has now been reached where there is real conflict between them and whether women are using this tension in any way. This raises an important issue for consideration in an empirical study of farm wives. How does women's access to, and participation in, paid employment affect the labour process and power relationships in the farm family? Indeed Delphy and Leonard acknowledge that earning an income does substantially improve a wife's bargaining power within the family. They draw on empirical studies of farm families in France to substantiate their theoretical position, arguing that farm families provide an interesting case for examination of women's work within the family, where a range of family members of both sexes work for the HOH producing goods and services for their own consumption and for the market. Even though farm wives produce so visibly for the market, they are just as subordinated as non-farm women because of the relations of production (the family) in which they live and work – they work unpaid for the HOH. Consumption within families is also unequal, with the HOH and older male children being more privileged than women or daughters. Transmission of property and resources favours men over women, particularly in farming where sons generally inherit the farm, but also because resources are distributed to individuals according to their status as persons, differentiated by age, sex and marital status.

Delphy and Leonard's work is unique and important in going beyond the labour and decision-making processes and examining transmission and consumption in order to reveal the gender-based structured inequalities within farm families. However, although they do show very clearly how transmission and consumption practices subordinate women and reinforce inequalities associated with the division of labour, and they do highlight important issues for empirical investigation, it is the labour process itself which they identify as the principal site of women's subordination. In this Delphy and Leonard seem in a sense trapped by the requirements of a materialist analysis, and specifically the need to establish that women's labour is exploited in the family 'mode of production'. This has the effect of creating a kind of reductionism by which women's influence on family processes can not be easily accommodated. By casting farm women primarily as workers for the HOH (whether on the farm or in the home), Delphy and Leonard leave very little theoretical space for women's impact on social reproduction, particularly their role as mothers through which they can influence children. In this sense, like other materialist analyses, their account cannot accommodate the dynamics of how women interpret, shape and construct the world around them (Finch, 1989; Cheal, 1991). More fundamentally the concepts of HOH and paid/unpaid work do not seem robust enough to carry such a large theoretical edifice, especially in farm families where payment does not come in the form of an individualised wage. Even if we accept that families are hierarchical in structure, Delphy and Leonard's descriptions of family processes (such as their description of the HOH as 'lord and master', 1992: 143–44) seem to greatly oversimplify the very complex processes involved in marital negotiation. This will be evident from the empirical data in later chapters.

Delphy and Leonard accept that their analysis does not take account of women's responses to the constraints associated with their subordination. Although they stress that they do not wish to portray women as colluding in their own oppression, the weight of their arguments does appear to leave little room for agency, so that women appear as 'victims, robots or fools' (Stacey, 1986). Such accounts can not address resistance to subordination or the specificity of local conditions and cultures. Yet women's resistance can affect not only their own lives in specific circumstances but also social formations in the wider society. Berlan Darque (1988) has noted a variety of responses among French farm women who have negotiated quite different sets of relationships within the confines of the patriarchal family farm, and in the process have gained considerable autonomy (1988: 228). Bouquet (1984) has also shown how the commercialisation of the domestic sphere – the taking in of visitors – ensures the reproduction of the farm household. Coleman and Elbert (1984) and Elbert (1988) have also elaborated the way in which farm women contest and cooperate at the same time, thus 'demonstrating a form of feminism that reaches beyond any simple definition of autonomy or individualism' (Elbert, 1988: 263).

Women, Farm and Family – The Present Study

The works of Hannan and Katsiaouni (1977), Whatmore (1991), and Delphy and Leonard (1992) provide the theoretical and empirical foundations for the present study. In exploring women' involvement in family farming in Ireland, I have drawn on the rich heritage of concepts and ideas in these studies and have sought to build on and expand their work in several ways. Firstly, while the labour process (the work that women do and the relations in which they work) is central to the analysis, women's involvement in consumption and reproduction are also included in the investigation. Consequently, the research investigates areas hitherto largely unexplored in studies of family farming. Secondly, the labour process and ownership and control of resources on the family farm are seen, not just as the nexus of patriarchal power relations, but also as part of a complex arena of negotiation involving women in different sets of relationships with the family farm. Thus, the nature of women's involvement and their own understanding of it will reflect not just the outcome of social relations which subordinate them, but their tactical responses to subordination through either cooperation or resistance.

Thirdly, there is considerable emphasis on trying to discover women's unique influence on the trajectory of family farming and its association with their past and present experience of the constraints of patriarchal structures. Women are seen as active agents in the restructuring of family farming as a social form, and also in the wider social formation – the evolution of Irish rural society. For this reason there is much greater attention given to reproduction, in so far as it is central both to understanding women's involvement in family farming and to the evolution of family farming itself. Consequently, farm women as mothers as well as wives are a central focus.

We have already mentioned above that, while the concept of production (involving the transformation of raw materials into goods for consumption or exchange) has been relatively unproblematic, that of 'reproduction' has been much more controversial. Friedmann defines reproduction as 'the renewal from one round of production to another of the social and technical elements of production and of the relations among them' (1981: 162). This definition seems too restrictive and static (Whatmore, 1991; Marsden, 1991) particularly since Friedmann appears to assume an equal commitment to the family farm among all family members (see especially Friedmann, 1986b: 51). Feminist theorists have used the concept of reproduction in a number of ways. Narrow definitions confine the concept to human reproduction – the reproduction of the species (McDonough and Harrison, 1978). Reproduction of labour (Mackintosh, 1981) involves the reproduction of people but not just biologically. It also involves the whole process of care and socialisation which ensures the continuation of society. Social reproduction is yet a wider concept which involves the process by which relations of production in society are perpetuated. Edholm et al. (1977) have argued that the three processes of biological reproduction, reproduction of the labour force and social reproduction must be kept analytically separate.

Whatever the problems and ambiguities surrounding the concept, reproduction is seen here as involving three separate but interrelated processes – reproduction of the family farm as an enterprise; reproduction of family farming as a social form; and social reproduction in the sense of reproduction of human society. The nature of women's involvement in these reproductive processes is a matter for empirical investigation as is the relationship between this involvement and the persistence of family farming.

Fourthly, the issues of power and influence are very much to the fore in this study, since women are seen as powerful actors in their own right. Following Giddens' conceptualisation of 'duality of structure', power is seen as intrinsically related to human agency so that it must, in this context, be treated as a 'transformative capacity' (1979: 92). This involves a move away from a coercive, absolutist idea of power to one of power as negotiation. No matter how repressive the structures under which the individual actor operates, the very idea of agency involves participation in the 'dialectic of control' whereby 'all power relations or relations of autonomy and dependence are reciprocal and, however wide the asymmetrical distribution of resources involved, all power relations manifest autonomy and dependence in "both directions"' (1979: 149). Thus, women cannot be seen as 'powerless victims'; there is always room to manoeuvre. This directly challenges the idea of conceptualising farm women as acquiescent merely because we can see their 'invisibility' (see Shortall, 1992). Indeed as Connell (1987: 111) has argued, there is evidence that domestic patriarchy (for instance) has been widely contested.

Finally, ideology and cultural prescription can be major tools of oppression. In this study ideologies and cultural practices are seen as powerful forces which limit and constrain women but which can also be shaped and influenced by them. However, it is important to distinguish between the micro-relationships of power at the level of the farm family and the macro-patriarchal structures of domination in the wider society. Thus the study focuses not just on the micro world of the farm family, but also where relevant, on the wider macro world of agriculture and Irish society generally.

3

RESEARCHING WOMEN IN FARM FAMILIES

Introduction

The theoretical approach to the study of women's involvement in family farming outlined at the end of Chapter Two had several implications for the kind of research methodology to be adopted in the present study. At the most fundamental level, the research strategy had to be able to provide answers to two fairly simple, but hitherto largely unexplored, questions: how can we understand women's involvement in family farming in Ireland; and what is the significance of this involvement for women themselves and for the future of family farming? The 'official' invisibility of farm women in family farming made it imperative that the research, and its interpretation, should be based as much as possible on women's own accounts of their lives. This would minimise the possibility of slippage into imposed categories (of work, for instance) and allow the social organisation of women's lives on family farms to emerge. Consequently, I felt that the research strategy should be such as to enable women to talk about their involvement in the farm family and the family farm. It also had to be sufficiently penetrating to allow for the interpretation of family processes and the significance of the 'family' in family farming. I concluded that this could best be achieved by documenting farm women's personal experiences of various aspects of everyday life including the negotiation of relationships within their families.

Secondly, given my objective of attempting to discover how women fare within the apparently patriarchal structures of family farming and how farm women influence the reproduction of this form of farming, the research design had to allow for connections to be made between the macro and micro levels. The relevant macro/micro conjunctions here are family farming as a form of production in capitalist agriculture as opposed to the micro level of the family farm, and the patriarchal structures of the wider society as opposed to the gender regime of the farm family. Thus my enquiry had to try to penetrate the 'black box' of the farm family and the complexities of the power relations within it, and attempt to make connections between this micro world and wider social relations.

Thirdly, it was necessary to take account of the very considerable regional differences in the character of agrarian restructuring in Ireland. As pointed out in Chapter One, both the material circumstances and the evolution of family farming among smallholders in the west of Ireland are quite different from those of the more commercial farms in the east and south. Thus, I considered it important to include women from contrasting regions. Fourthly, I wished to take into consideration the feminist critique of much social science research as being androcentric and unable to comprehend the complexities of women's lives. This critique has led many academic feminists to adapt or abandon conventional survey methods in order to allow the subjects' voices to be heard more clearly and to acknowledge the validity of accounts of lived experience as research data. Finally, the method adopted had to be practical and feasible for a lone researcher with limited resources. Taking all of these considerations into account in organising a research strategy presented a number of challenges.

Research Challenges

Farm Women as Subjects – Action and Structure

Intellectual conviction, experience, and instinct convinced me that the key to understanding the kinds of social processes with which the study was concerned lay in adopting an 'actor-oriented' approach. Oakley (1992), in her fascinating reflections on the research process, argues that the goal of scientific research is not knowing but understanding. While the requirements of social science knowledge might be satisfied by quantifiable data, understanding can only be obtained by attention to subjective narrative. It is out of the dialectic between knowledge and understanding that research findings are produced. It seemed to me that any attempt to know and understand women's predicament within farm families had to begin with the assumption of women as active agents. This is not to overlook the importance of structure but to argue that an actor-oriented approach grounded in the everyday life experiences of farm women would best capture the variety of meanings and strategies with which they interpret and deal with their social world. Long (1990,

1992) has been one of the main advocates in rural sociology of this approach to understanding change and continuity, arguing that it is the interplay of actor strategies and individual and collective 'projects' which generate social forms, which in turn shape future possibilities for action. Villarreal has usefully described this process as follows:

> Society is composed of actors, thinking agents, capable of strategizing and finding space for manoeuvre in the situations they face and manipulating resources and constraints. Economic and political considerations, as well as life experiences and particular everyday circumstances, are relevant to the way actors tie together, act upon, attribute meaning to, and recreate different elements. (1992: 248)

This is not to say that structure is unimportant or to underplay the importance of macro-phenomena, but to suggest that apprehension of social processes at the micro level is a first step to understanding action. One way of finding out how people make sense of the world around them is to talk to them about it. The crux of the matter is then a question of how the actions of individuals are to be related to the wider social order, i.e., the relationship between micro and macro social processes. Giddens (1976: 121) has attempted to resolve this problem through his concept of duality of structure in which social structures are constituted by human agency and at the same time are the very medium of this constitution. In *New Rules of Sociological Method* he makes three points which are central to the approach in the present study: firstly, the need to understand action as *Praxis* (people are involved in actions to realise their interests); secondly, that power is central to social life; and thirdly, social norms or rules are capable of different interpretation by social actors (Giddens, 1976: 53, emphasis in original).

Notwithstanding the patriarchal structures of family farming, it seemed then that the study should begin from the premise that women in farm families must be seen as actors with interests, rather than as hapless (or helpless) victims of what Oakley calls the fallacies of capitalism and the phallacies of patriarchy (1992: ix). Moreover, asymmetrical power relations as they operate at the micro level of the farm family needed to be examined and understood, both in terms of their source within the family and in relation to the wider context of subordination and domination, that is, to gender relations in society generally. Giddens' third point above suggests that the way in which farm women as actors interpret and make sense of the social world will be influenced by their experiences in a society and social form (family farming) which is structured on the basis of gender. Their responses to these experiences will in turn shape and change gendered structures.

Even though Irish farm families have been an object of study, and some research has been carried out on farm women's contribution to the farm business (Hannan and Katsiaouni, 1977; Gasson, 1992), Irish farm women as such have never been the specific object of study. Shortall (1992) did focus her research on farm wives but her primary interest was in exploring theories of power. She treated farm women as a particular case for an empirical test of a theory of power. Their involvement in family farming and their understanding of it have never been researched in a systematic way, despite their pivotal position within farm families.

My immediate research focus then would be at the 'micro level' of the family farm and the farm family. Knorr-Cetina (1981) has put forward the concept of methodological situationalism as a way of linking micro and macro sociological perspectives, arguing that it is through micro-social approaches that we learn most about the macro order. She emphasises the importance of conceptualising power at the micro level and uses the example of family violence to explain her idea that the exercise of power is part of the routine of everyday transactions (1981: 23). Given my concern with attempting to understand the reality of farm women's daily existence within the constraints of farm and family structures in which power relations are central, I considered that questioning women about the daily realities of their lives should be at the core of the research. Here it might be possible to discern ways in which women are constrained; how they act to further their interests; whether/how they resist and contest power; and the sources of their own power and influence. Such micro-level data could be supplemented by macro-level data where necessary. The point is to understand women's actions in their day-to-day lives and how they are linked to wider structural outcomes.

A Qualitative Approach

Knorr-Cetina's work is part of a wider and ongoing debate concerning the focus of sociological investigation, i.e., whether it should be at the macro or micro level, and whether qualitative or quantitative methods should be used (see Cicourel, 1981; Collins, 1981; Fielding, 1988). A frequent contention in these debates is that the aggregation and classification associated with quantitative methods such as in large-scale surveys, together with the sacrifice of context which this necessitates, is problematic. As Cicourel points out, the analytic categories derived from survey data are potentially mere artefacts of the analytic procedure itself. Collective entities are created out of distributions by income, class, education or occupation that have no actual existence which can be studied by other means. In short, surveys are rarely supplemented by analyses at the micro level which reflect the lived existence of the individuals being studied (1981: 65). Brannen has argued that the primary difference between the two methods is in the way they treat data. Qualitative research is theoretical in its aims; it is the development and testing of theory that is important rather than measurement, inference or generalisability. She sees the qualitative researcher as looking through 'a wide lens, searching for patterns of inter-relationships between a previously unspecified set of concepts, while the quantitative researcher looks through a narrow lens at a specified set of variables' (1992: 4).

Recently, several writers have put forward the view that the qualitative/quantitative division is misleading and restrictive and has led to an undue separation of methods when in fact many researchers have combined them quite effectively. They maintain that as research strategies, qualitative and quantitative methods can be detached from the epistemological and theoretical concerns which set them apart. These writers advocate 'multi-method' (Bryman, 1988; Hammersley, 1992a) or 'multi-strategy' (Layder, 1993) approaches to data collection, taking into account the practical issues such as the time and research funding available. They are refreshingly frank about the practical dilemmas of data gathering, in a way hitherto usually only found in feminist discourse. Layder (1993) has stressed the importance of using quantitative data to complement qualitative fieldwork. This is not to argue that macro-phenomena are essentially quantitative, but that quantitative measures may provide indicators of the shape of macro-processes. The measurable 'invisibility' of women in the public world of agriculture is a case in point.

Feminist reflections on social science have provided trenchant critiques of mainstream research methods, epistemology, and theory, and offered alternative feminist perspectives (Eichler, 1980; Stanley and Wise, 1983; Harding, 1987; Stanley, 1990; Thompson, 1992). Partly because of the way that conventional measures (of work, and social class for instance) in large-scale quantitative research have ignored or misrepresented women's concerns, many feminists have shunned the survey method altogether, opting instead for ethnographic methods, case studies, life histories or discourse analysis. Feminists have argued that research strategies which adopt a 'scientific', positivistic mode of enquiry cannot possibly explore the meanings and social processes which are at the core of human experience. According to Mies (1983), a feminist research agenda should include women's social history, their perception of their situation, women's subordination, and how it is contested and resisted. Devault has argued persuasively that feminist researchers need to:

take responsibility for recognizing how the concepts we have learned as sociologists may distort women's accounts. We can return to activities conducted in specific settings as the sources for our studies, and ground our interviewing in accounts of everyday activity – in accounts of how particular women actually spend their time at home, for example, rather than a previously defined concept of 'housework'. (1990: 101)

While there is still much debate about the nature and boundaries of feminist methodology (see Hammersley, 1992b; Ramazanoglu, 1992; Gelsthorpe, 1992; Lentin, 1993; Mahon, 1994), the theoretical approach taken here is very much influenced by feminist theory which posits an explicit relationship between gender and power. This implies a particular methodological strategy in order to apprehend women's experience of gendered power relationships. A notable body of work has accumulated over the past twenty years (not all of it explicitly feminist) which has provided valuable insights into women's lives and family processes by the use of small-scale studies involving interviews with women. These include, inter alia, Oakley's work on housework (1974) and childbirth (1980), Leonard's study of courtship (1980), Boulton's work on motherhood (1983), Finch on wives' relationship to their husband's job (1983) and O'Connor on women's close relationships (1990, 1992).

My own experiences of doing both ethnographic and survey research on Irish farms had led me to realise the limitations and advantages of different approaches. While a large-scale survey of farm women might provide useful baseline data, I knew it would yield little in terms of helping to understand the meanings which farm women attach to their lives. Also, since I would be unable to do all the interviewing myself, I would be very much removed from the research subjects and would have to rely on normative definitions of such commonplace, but in this context critical, concepts as 'work'. An ethnographic approach, on the other hand, would confine my investigation to one locality when I believed it was important to try to have a somewhat broader focus. Experience of both researching Irish farming and living in rural Ireland convinced me that my main objective of exploring with farm women the context and meaning of their lives could best be achieved by in-depth interviews with a cross-section of such women.

Which Farm Women? The Regional Issue

The decision to base the research on detailed personal interviews with farm women raised the issue of how to select them. Clearly women could be selected on the basis of farm (e.g., size of enterprise, system of farming, pluriactivity) or individual characteristics (e.g., women's age, occupational status, generation). However, given my concern with linking women's involvement in family farming with the reproduction of this form of farming, I felt that I should take account of regional differences. As pointed out in earlier chapters, agrarian change and rural restructuring in Ireland has quite a different character in the more disadvantaged farming areas of the west and north-west compared to the commercial farming areas of the east and south. Moreover, the wider research project with which this study was associated could provide useful contextual data for the west and east regions (see below). Previous experience of conducting research on farms in the west had given me a considerable understanding of the situation of farming families there. I had earlier carried out two studies of socio-economic and structural changes in farming and farm households in the west region during the 1970s and 1980s, involving both qualitative and quantitative research methods (Kelleher and O'Hara, 1978; Conway and O'Hara, 1984; O'Hara, 1985). Indeed, as was pointed out in Chapter Two, the west of Ireland has a much richer heritage of both anthropological and sociological research than the east. The fact that I did not have the same familiarity with the east (through the literature or from personal experience), seemed to be both an advantage (I would be less influenced by prior assumptions) and a disadvantage (less familiarity with the cultural and social environment). Either way, it seemed important to capture the differences by including women from both regions, particularly since comparatively little was known about the reproduction of family farming in the more commercial farming areas of the east. I decided therefore to interview an equal number of women from areas in the west and east.

The Research Process

Selection of Households

The sixty women eventually selected for interview were from households in two areas: one in the west, which included counties Mayo, Galway and Roscommon; and the other in the east, covering counties Dublin, Louth, Meath, Kildare and Wicklow. These farm households were selected from a larger sample of almost six hundred farm households which were participants in a wider Irish survey, which in turn was part of an EU-wide study.[1] The wider survey provided important base-

1. This study was part of a twelve nation European research project on farm structures and pluriactivity (see Arkleton Trust, 1992). The Irish part of the study was undertaken by Teagasc (Agricultural and Food Development Authority).

line data for the selection of farm households for my study, and also a broader context (subject to the limitations of the data, since the wider study was concerned with changes in farm structures and pluriactivity, rather than farm women or intra-family processes) within which to locate the more detailed analysis. Of the 600 farms[2] in the wider study, 300 each were located in the west and east. The completed survey had yielded 291 interviews in the west and 274 in the east. A sub-sample or panel of 120 farm households (sixty in each location) had been selected for more detailed annual interviews over a three year period. These 'panel' households had been chosen from the larger sample using a selection procedure common to all the study areas in the EU research project. Purposive sampling had been used to ensure representation of the variety of different conditions in family farming, particularly in relation to pluriactivity and commitment to farming (see Arkleton Trust, 1992). I was fortunate in having access to the resulting data sets which I have used in a number of ways.

Firstly, I selected my sixty interviewees from the 120 'panel farm households'. The selection process began with an analysis of the existing interview data from the panel households. This allowed me to construct a profile of each of the 120 farms. These profiles included characteristics of the farm enterprise and current farming activity; the household structure, including basic data on each household member; pluriactivity in the farm household; and the future prospects for the farm enterprise. I then began a process of selecting households for the present study. Since farm women as wives/mothers comprise the majority of all farm women, and since the farm family was a major focus of the research, only farm households in which there was (or had recently been) a farm couple with or without children (not necessarily resident) were included. The 'farm wife' (as opposed to the farm woman who was unmarried) was the intended respondent and I have used this term 'farm wife' (reluctantly, but in preference to farmer's wife) throughout the study. Households in which there was no appropriate woman resident, single-person households, or households in which the relevant woman was aged over seventy were omitted. In an earlier round of interviews for the wider survey, potential respondents had been asked for their cooperation with my study and those who indicated an unwillingness to cooperate were eliminated.

The sixty completed interviews reflect these pragmatic considerations. There was only one farm woman who refused to be interviewed.

2. This involved a two-stage sampling procedure by which farms were selected from clusters of District Electoral Divisions. A questionnaire was administered to each of these households by personal interview in 1987 and 1991.

In one other case an interview had to end somewhat prematurely because of the unexpected and aggressive interruption by the interviewee's husband who virtually ordered me off the farm. However, since I had already carried out a lengthy interview at that point, I have included the material in the study. I included three recently widowed women in the east and one in the west because I considered that their experiences might be able to provide different and valuable insights into some of the issues which I was investigating.

Apart from enabling me to construct a profile of each farm household prior to interviewing the farm woman, the fact that their households were included in the wider study meant that I also had an opportunity to talk to the interviewers who had already visited these households. The earlier interviews were usually conducted with the male 'farm operator' but wives or adult children were sometimes interviewed instead. Discussions with these interviewers provided me with invaluable background and contextual information so that I had considerable knowledge of each household before I began to talk to the farm woman. Finally, although the data set from the survey had a much broader focus and much of the detailed data on farm production was unsuitable for my purposes, it did provide a wider context in which to locate the farm families studied and a potential to link micro and macro data. In the analysis in the following chapters, I have been able to use the wider survey information to try to bridge the macro-micro gulf, not always successfully, but as a way of validating the insights gained in the personal interviews and advancing the theoretical arguments. Before turning to a discussion of the interviewing process, the areas in which the study farms are located are briefly described.

The Study Areas

The western counties are part of a region west of the river Shannon where the farm holdings are generally small, with much of the land in poor quality rough pasture. This region has been designated a Less Favoured Area by the EU. Cattle and sheep production are the dominant enterprises and farming is small scale and generally less intensive than in the more specialised tillage and dairy farming areas in the south and east. The proportion engaged in farming has been consistently among the highest in the EU. The region has a long history of out-migration reflecting the lack of non-farm employment opportunities there.

The eastern counties by contrast are around the perimeter of Dublin. Farms there are generally larger and the land is more fertile than in the west. Tillage farming is more prevalent as is market gardening which supplies fruit and vegetables to the Dublin market. Being in the general Dublin catchment area, these counties have not suffered population losses but have had a net inflow of people through migration from the more remote rural areas and through suburbanisation. Dependence on agricultural employment in these counties is half that of the west region at fifteen percent. The general economic environment is far more dynamic and diversified with associated opportunities for non-agricultural employment.

The regional differences in farm size and farming systems are evident from the wider survey (Tables 3.1 and 3.2). Only 40 percent of farms in the west exceed twenty hectares, compared to almost 60 percent in the east. While cattle and sheep production are the most important enterprises on the majority of farms in both areas, dairying is the only other significant enterprise in the west. In the east, more than a fifth of farms have either tillage or market gardening as their most important enterprise.

In terms of the sources of income available to farm families, the main difference between the two areas is in the number of households which have an income from social transfers (Table 3.3). Almost two thirds of farm households in the west had an income from this source, compared to just a fifth in the east.

Table 3.1
Distribution of Farms by Size of Holding in the West and East in the Wider Survey

Farm Size (UAA)[1] (Hectares)	West (%)	East (%)
0 – <10	6.2	15.7
10 – <20	54.0	26.6
20 – <50	30.6	23.4
50 +	9.2	34.3
Total	100.0	100.0
N	291	274

Source: Teagasc, internal files.
Note: 1. Utilised Agricultural Area. Includes area under crops, pasture and rough grazing, net of land rented or let, or used for non-agricultural purposes

Table 3.2

Most Important Enterprise on Farms in the West and East in the Wider Survey

Enterprise	West (%)	East (%)
Cattle	58.3	42.9
Dairying	13.3	15.3
Sheep	27.4	19.3
Tillage	1.0	17.0
Market Gardening	0.0	5.5
Total	100.0	100.0
N	285	254

Source: Teagasc, internal files.

Table 3.3

Sources of Income in Farm Households in the Wider Survey

Sources of Income [1]	West (%)	East (%)
Farming	100.0	100.0
Off-farm work of operator	23.0	25.5
Off-farm work of spouse	15.1	14.6
Off-farm work of other family members	18.9	21.2
Social transfers	65.6	20.8
N	291	274

Source: Teagasc, internal files.

Note: 1. The numbers of households in which the operator and/or spouse had an off-farm job are exaggerated, especially in the east, as pluriactivity was a criterion for the selection of households. In Ireland in 1990, an estimated 21 percent of farm operators and 16 percent of spouses had off-farm jobs (Power and Roche, 1991). Unfortunately, we do not have comparable data from the counties included in the survey. However, data from the 1994 National Farm Survey revealed that 21 and 12 percent of farm holders and spouses respectively had off-farm jobs in the 'East' with comparable figures for the 'West' at 27 and 17 percent. 'East' and 'West' are not directly comparable with east and west as defined in the present study.

The Interviews

The interviews were conducted between April and December 1991. Appointments were arranged in advance as the women lived in widely scattered locations. The study was explained to the respondents as constituting a follow-up to the wider survey discussed above, pointing out that in this case I was concerned with the lives of women on farms and their views about a range of issues. Each interview covered a specific range of topics arising from the concepts and ideas discussed in the Chapter Two. These included: the woman's own background; the circumstances of her entry into farming; her work on the farm, in the household, and off the farm; sharing arrangements in the family, particularly as regards money and the care of children; details on the children themselves; and the future of the family farm. While these topics provided the core themes for the interviews, they were mainly used more as guides to conversation so that they facilitated, rather than restricted, spontaneous opinions and comments from the interviewees. Interviews lasted about two hours on average but ranged in length from one and a half to three hours. Just under a third of the women interviewed were aged forty or under, 43 percent were aged between 41 and 55, and the remaining quarter were aged over 56. The youngest interviewee was aged twenty-three and the oldest sixty-six.

Oakley (1974) has pointed out that in the rapport between interviewer and interviewee, there is a sense of sharing in the 'community of women'; and a sense of dialogue rather than subject/object encounter are inherent parts of the interview process. The atmosphere at the interviews was very much conditioned by farm women's eagerness to talk. Almost without exception, they relished the opportunity to have a listener who appeared genuinely interested in the reality of their lives. Finch (1984) and Oakley (1992) have described their experiences of interviewing in similar terms, with Finch titling her article on the subject 'It's great to have someone to talk to' – a sentiment which was frequently expressed by the farm women interviewed for this study. My own disposition during the interviews was to create an environment in which the women felt secure; where they saw me as someone who was genuinely interested in their view of the world rather than just a collector of information. Thus, I accepted offers of tea with most of the women or (more unusually) talked to them as they worked and responded carefully when they asked me for my opinion. I ran errands where they were needed or provided information when requested (about welfare entitlement for instance). In many cases I listened to stories of illness and family problems which had nothing to do with the study but which I regarded as an important way of establishing trust and respect between interviewer and interviewee. Most women were interviewed alone, but in some cases children were present or the respondent's husband arrived during the course of the interview. Early on I took the difficult decision not to use a tape-recorder, as I knew from past experience of fieldwork in the west of Ireland and also from interviewing for radio broadcasts, how the presence of a tape-recorder can alter and inhibit responses. The most interesting information often emerges when the tape-recorder has been turned off and then it is not possible to take notes, as the respondent assumes the conversation is 'off the record'. Moreover, farm families in Ireland have a strong wish for privacy, wariness of formal questions, and little experience of tape-recorded interviews. For these reasons I judged that I would be likely to elicit more frank and open responses about family processes (such as ways of handling money) if I took notes instead. I was also particularly careful about assurances of confidentiality. I therefore openly took detailed notes and immediately after the completion of each interview transcribed the entire contents into a portable personal computer. In this way I was able to capture the full richness of the interviews virtually verbatim. The method I adopted lengthened the interviewing period greatly, because of the time taken to interview and transcribe on the same day. On the other hand I had the advantage of being continually confronted with the data which enabled me to build and refine my observations and questions as I went along.

The analysis in the following chapters is based primarily on the interview material from the farm women.[3] However, in each chapter the women's accounts have been supplemented by relevant macro data either from the wider survey or from secondary sources. This approach to presenting the material evolved out of the process of data interpretation and the organisation of the interview material. Even at an early stage, certain patterns in the circumstances of farm women's lives and their accounts of their experiences began to emerge and these became clearer as I continued to sort and organise the interview material. I have tried to present the data in a way that uses farm women's voices as much as possible but also tries to locate their accounts within a context and framework which can sometimes be presented quantitatively, or used to validate interpretations based on qualitative material. While I do not wish to claim that the interpretations can be generalised to all farm women in Ireland, I have tried to relate women's actions and everyday experience to wider social processes such as emigration and educational attainment. I do not see this research as just being 'about' or 'on' women but as part of the recent tradition of research 'for' women (Thompson, 1992). In seeking to make farm women visible, I have tried not just to document inequalities but to show women as active agents within the confines of the farm family/family farm even if 'not in conditions of their own choosing'.

3. The text quotes from the interviewees are referenced by the letter E or W to distinguish between east and west, and numbered 1 to 30 in each area. The references are supplemented by other information where relevant. The letter 'H' is used to refer to respondents' husbands throughout.

4

CREATING THE FARM FAMILY

Becoming a Farm Wife

Introduction

A fundamental requirement for the reproduction of family farming is the constitution and reconstitution of farm families through marriage. Among prospective marriage partners, the male is usually the actual or potential farmer, since only in exceptional circumstances do women acquire farms by gift, inheritance or otherwise. The predominance of male inheritance and ownership of land and capital determines that women enter farming on unequal material terms with their husbands, unless they possess comparable capital in terms of land, property, or earning power. Marriage is a crucial mechanism for change and continuity among farm families, and studies of Irish rural life and family farming have consistently emphasised its importance. Arensberg and Kimball saw marriage as combining 'transfer of economic control, land ownership, reformation of family ties, advance in family and community status and entrance into adult procreative sex life. It is a central focus of rural life, a universal turning point in individual histories' (1968: 103).

When Arensberg and Kimball carried out their study in the 1930s, 'matchmaking' was the predominant way of arranging marriage among the families of smallholders. The 'match' was initiated by the prospective bridegroom's father, while the future bride's father decided on the size of her 'fortune' or dowry. Marriage was primarily an economic arrangement, the outcome of a bargain between male farmers. Their sons and daughters were relatively passive participants in the bargaining process in which the continuity and integrity of the family holding were the paramount interests. When love or attraction threatened to bring aspiring mates together independent of a match, unwanted complications were created (Arensberg and Kimball, 1968: 114). The practice of matchmaking has now disappeared and contemporary farm marriages involve ideas of romantic love and free choice. Nevertheless, marriage remains materially significant and is contracted in the context of a cultural heritage in which family loyalties, security of property and subordination of women were dominant features. Farm marriage is fundamentally about property and kinship, involving the creation of a new farm family where biological reproduction will ensure the continuity of family farming as a social form. For individual women and men, it is also about the selection of a partner, a co-parent for potential children, the establishment of a home, and the sharing of a way of life. While the formation of the nuclear family is clearly critical to farm continuity, the existence of a nuclear farm family of parents and children has also been seen as strongly linked to farm viability (Scully, 1971; Symes, 1972). During the 1970s, concern about the links between family structure and level of output on Irish farms even led to the use of the term 'bad demography' to describe single person or single generation households, and 'bad demography' was shown to be associated with low farm output and income (Johnson and Conway, 1976). Conway (1976: 90) argued that family viability is a crucial factor in determining the output on Irish farms. Indeed the National Farm Survey continues to use 'demography' (a synonym for family structure) as a factor in estimating the viability of Irish farms (Power and Roche, 1995).

Clearly then, women are essential to the formation, viability and continuity of family farms, but their significance has been acknowledged only indirectly in studies of farm production and the restructuring of agriculture. This is usually through consideration of demographic factors associated with the household structure, such as the absence of visible successors because of bachelorhood or childless marriages. The issue of whether there is any connection between such demographic features and women's status in family farming has not been addressed. Indeed the very discourse of the links between household demographic structure and farm viability is gender blind (see Scully's discussion of 'one-man farms', 1971: 68–69). While the absence of women has long been clearly identified as a critical factor associated with low farm incomes, farm viability and dissolution of smallholdings, this has not translated into serious investigation and definition of either the status of farm wives or the significance of their input to farm production. It is as if there is a presumed equality and unity of interest within the farm family which makes irrelevant any consideration of the status of farm women and its relationship to viability or continuity. On the other hand, studies which have attempted to understand and explain Ireland's unusual demographic patterns of late marriage, permanent celibacy, and migration from rural areas, have acknowledged the significance of gender differences in rural social processes. Women's subordinate status within family farming and in rural social life has been associated with these demographic features. This literature has shown how women resisted the strictures of family farming and rural life and avoided marriage to farmers, by migrating out of rural areas (Kennedy, 1973; Fitzpatrick, 1986; Moser, 1993; Travers, 1995). Women's actions had, in this way, a profound influence on the demographic and social structure of rural Ireland.

This chapter then is about marriage, and it has four main sections. Firstly, Ireland's distinctive demographic patterns are linked to women's resistance to the highly patriarchal nature of Irish family farming which resulted in the majority of farm daughters leaving rural Ireland and eschewing marriage to farmers. In the following section the farm women in the study become the focus of attention and their backgrounds, educational and occupational characteristics are examined. This provides both a context for the study as a whole and a backdrop for an examination of the circumstances of marriage which are addressed in the third section. Two particular situations – where women married from home and where they returned from abroad to marry – provide striking evidence of the very limited choices which these women actually had. They also reveal the strength of cultural and ideological values associated with family farming, particularly as they translate into family obligation. However, the fact that some women were prepared to marry into farming did not mean that they unquestioningly accepted its strictures upon themselves. The fact that they were exceptional in becoming farm wives, in a situation where most women were avoiding such marriages, was in itself a source of empowerment, allowing them some leverage to challenge and contest patriarchal structures. The cultural differences between west and east emerge clearly here and in the fourth section, where women's accounts of the early years of marriage show how they negotiated and contested the patriarchal structures of family farming. Their actions are bringing about a reshaping of ideologies of marriage and family which are reflected in the lives of younger farm wives.

Women's Aversion to Farm and Rural Life

In order to understand the relationship between women's actions and demographic patterns, it is necessary to refer briefly to mid-nineteenth century Ireland when a number of changes occurred which adversely affected the status of farm women. The establishment of the stem family system of impartible inheritance after the great famine, required 'brutally clear-cut distinctions' to be made among sons, and between sons and daughters (Hannan, 1979: 40). The stem family system involved the transfer of the farm intact to a sole male heir, and women inherited farms only in exceptional circumstances. It allowed the possibility of creating a farm family for (on average) only two of the offspring of any farm couple – the son who would inherit the farm and a daughter who would marry another local heir. In this context marriage took on a new significance and matchmaking and the dowry system reinforced male dominance. In this period too, women's economic position was weakened by the contraction of domestic industry, so that the late nineteenth century has been described as a 'dismal' period for Irish women (Fitzpatrick, 1986).

For the century after the famine, life for women on Irish farms was particularly harsh and unrelenting, involving much physical labour and the least entitlement to nutritious food. Such conditions even led to their premature deaths. Kennedy (1973: 6), comparing mortality rates by sex, nationality, rural urban residence, age, and cause of death, found that 'the subordinate status of Irish females did increase their mortality levels from what they might otherwise have been'. He attributes Irish women's vulnerability to a number of factors which were associated with their subordinate status:

> The less adequate diet given to females in many Irish families probably contributed to the lower resistance of females to infectious and parasitic diseases. Malnutrition and fatigue resulting from continued heavy workloads also probably explained at least part of the more rapid ageing of Irish females. Rural housewives in other countries also experienced some loss of longevity for these reasons, but compared with the United States and several northwest European countries in the twentieth century, the Irish pattern was extreme. (Kennedy, 1973: 63–64)

AE (G.W. Russell), observing the situation in 1912, tried to capture what a young Irish woman might have felt as she 'looked on the wrinkled face and bent back and rheumatic limbs of her mother, and grown maddened in a sudden passion that her own fresh young life might end just like this'(AE 1912: 66, quoted in Lee, 1989).

Escape Strategies

Irish women's subordinate status was literally killing them and, from the late nineteenth century onwards, they responded to these harsh conditions in two ways which were interconnected. Firstly, they left rural Ireland and migrated to the cities. Guinnane has shown how, in the first decade of the twentieth century, farm daughters were more likely to leave home and to do so earlier than sons (1992: 652). Women migrated even if this lessened their possibilities of finding a marriage partner, since single women outnumbered men in urban areas. Emigration from Ireland, which was mainly to the United States and Britain, also contained a relatively higher proportion of females (Kennedy, 1973: 84). Indeed, although there were some fluctuations, over the period between 1871 and 1971 net female emigration exceeded that of males (Travers, 1995).

Education was the second avenue for improvement in women's status so that by the standards of the time they were better educated than their male counterparts. Fitzpatrick, writing about conditions in the late nineteenth century observed:

> Irish women took full advantage of the two means by which they could hope to improve their condition in life beyond that of their mothers. By the end of the century they were slightly better educated and more migratory than men, and their subsequent performance in the examination hall and foreign labour market was also superior. (Fitzpatrick, 1986: 225)

These two escape strategies tended to converge, in that better educated women were more likely to migrate. Decades later Hannan, in his study of rural migration in the 1960s, attributed females' greater propensity to leave rural areas to the higher levels of education received by girls, which were associated with their aspirations to higher status jobs not available locally (1970: 224–25).[1] More recently, Moser (1993: 44–45) has pointed out that, despite the availability of employment opportunities in the west of Ireland in the 1940s, women persisted in emigrating.

Women's rejection of rural life was a matter of concern to the government Commission on Emigration which was established in 1948. While mainly advocating the need for male employment creation to stem emigration, the Commission, in analysing the reasons for the low rates of marriage in Ireland's rural areas, recognised, somewhat grudgingly, the links with women's status and aspirations. Thus it acknowledged that facilitating women to retain employment after marriage might encourage more of them to remain in rural areas and marry, since they would be able to maintain, to some degree, their pre-marriage standard of living and have greater security. However, the Commission warned that this might result in a decrease in the fertility rate and that 'the effect on the home and the family has also to be remembered'

---

1. Mothers, of course, played a pivotal role in shaping daughters' aspirations and this will be discussed in detail in Chapter Seven.

(1954: 81). Nevertheless, however unwillingly, it did recognise that demographic patterns were connected to women's response to their status and the constraints of custom and culture, commenting on 'the disinclination on the part of many young girls to undertake the arduous duties of a farmer's wife and to accept the conditions of country life. Partly as a consequence of this, but also because of the opportunities for employment in towns, young girls leave farming areas, and hence there is a marked disproportion there between the numbers of males and females' (1954: 82).

Women's attempts to improve their status through acquiring education, and their associated aspirations to occupations not available locally, meant that they left rural areas in large numbers never to return. Rejection of the life that they had seen their mothers experience was bound up with an unwillingness to replicate that life by marrying a farmer (Travers, 1995: 196). They avoided marriage to farmers, even at the cost of remaining single, not only because of what they saw as the drudgery of farm life but also because by migrating they became part of a new urban culture. This in turn increased the social distance between them and the farmers' sons at home. They came to expect certain standards of behaviour, courtesy and refinement from potential partners and if these were not forthcoming from farmers, they were disinclined to consider them as potential husbands. McNabb writing of county Limerick in the early 1960s observed:

> The modern country girl is turning away from the land. The wealth of the prospective husband although still important is not so decisive as his personal appearance, his manners, and the kind of home he can provide. She objects to the 'muck and dirt' of the farm life and would prefer to marry a professional man or even a white collar worker. (1964: 221)

For women who had migrated, returning to live in a rural area frequently meant a reduction in their standard of living, having to carry out hard physical work on the family farm to which they had no ownership rights, fewer amenities, and a domestic arrangement which involved shared living accommodation with their husband's family. Having been raised on farms themselves, they were familiar with the reality of the life of the farm woman – they had seen their mothers working hard. For women in paid employment, marriage to a farmer usually meant having to relinquish one's pre-marriage occupation, with a consequent lowering in standard of living as well as the loss of financial independence, unless one was fortunate enough to make an exceptionally good match. Brody, writing of the decline of small farm communities in the west of Ireland observed that for 'a majority of the generation of young women just leaving school and deciding their futures, the prospect of marriage in the countryside is too absurd to consider. . . The women will not tolerate the demands which farm life imposes on them' (1973: 129).

So great were the numbers of rural women who moved to the cities that there were not enough single men available there for them to marry. Thus many women remained unmarried in urban areas both in Ireland and abroad, settling for such a status rather than marriage on a farm (Kennedy, 1973: 170). At the same time the proportions of farmers who never married continued to increase, particularly among those on smaller holdings. Only among farmers with more than forty hectares did the proportions unmarried decrease between 1946 and 1966. By 1981 more than a third of all farmers aged between 45 and 54 were unmarried. Those on small farms found it particularly difficult to find wives, which Breen et al. attribute not to the unwillingness of the men to marry but to the 'propensity of their sisters to escape as early as possible from such economically deprived backgrounds' (1990: 113).

Regional Differences

These trends did not develop uniformly in time or space. The stem family remained stronger and more resilient for longer on small farms with poor land in the west of Ireland than in other regions, even though these farms had the lowest incomes and standards of living. Demographic changes, characterised by low replacement and falling marriage rates, occurred earlier in the richer farming areas of the east and midlands and were significantly associated with class differences (Hannan, 1979). In 1926 less than ten percent of households in the west failed to replace themselves; in the east the non-replacement rate was almost three times as high. Over the next forty years this situation was reversed, so that by 1971 the smaller farms in the west had the highest incidence of non-replacement as measured by the proportions of older farmers who remained unmarried. Hannan acknowledges that 'disillusionment with subsistence farming had spread more rapidly and at an earlier date amongst farmers' daughters than farmers' sons', and that this happened in all regions (1979: 54). However, although he accepts that women's actions may have affected male farmers' marriage chances, his main argument is based on an assumption of male action as being at the core of the social processes associated with the reproduction of family farming.

In the west of Ireland, in the post-war period, what Hannan characterises as a unique peasant culture with a distinct set of values which had been described earlier by Arensberg and Kimball, and which was 'at odds

with the large commercial farming classes of the east and midlands',
began to collapse (1979: 65). He attributes this to the modernisation
and commercialisation of agriculture which led to increased income differentiation among the farm population. As a result smallholders became
more marginalised and impoverished. The demographic viability of the
west relative to the east was reversed so that the demoralisation and dis-
illusion that Brody (1973) witnessed in the west in the 1970s was the
outcome of a period of rapid decline over the previous two decades. As
Hannan put it:

> The situation by then had changed dramatically for the small western farm-
> ers, from one of a viable subsistence system to that of residual status. Nowa-
> days, crude market forces are being directly reflected in the subjective
> reactions of the small farming class. Previously it is quite apparent that, if
> anything, the objectively poorer the situation, the subjectively more 'opti-
> mistic' was the response. Different value standards were being employed in
> the east and west in the 1920s and 1930s. Now the same reference standards
> seem to be universally shared. (1979: 65)

In the west then, while disillusionment with their potential life chances
had led farm daughters to migrate in large numbers for decades, some of
their sisters had remained and married farm sons. Since the 'viable subsistence system' described by Hannan was based on male supremacy,
such daughters were effectively trapped by the reproductive imperative
of the stem family and the patriarchal authority which ensured its continuance. The majority of marriages were arranged, with the women
concerned having relatively little say in the marriage arrangement, while
their sisters were free to leave (Beal, 1986). Hannan regards such an efficient system of marriage as the hallmark of a form of peasant culture in
which the stem family system was preserved intact and non-inheriting
siblings dispersed. Indeed the very fact that the peasant economy was so
closed allowed it to retain a structure of parental authority which was
strongly patriarchal. In the years after the Second World War the gradual erosion of the peasant economy weakened that authority structure,
so that the last remaining farm daughter, aided and abetted by her
mother, felt free to leave home without guilt (Brody, 1973).

It is clear then that women's resistance to marriage to farmers, as
expressed in high female migration and low farmer marriage rates,
threatened the reproduction of family farming. Although this was not
the only reason for low marriage rates among farmers, it was among the
most significant. Others factors included enforced postponement of
marriage associated with late inheritance, the reduction in standard of
living associated with marriage and the influence of mothers of young

heirs, who may have discouraged their sons from marrying in order to retain their own domestic supremacy. Marriage as a strategy for social reproduction (Bourdieu, 1972), based as it was on male predominance (in terms of inheritance of patrimony and control over land resources), was not universally effective. Many women simply avoided marriage to farmers, particularly those on small holdings. There are however clear differences between west and east in the timing and character of agrarian restructuring which are reflected in the contemporary marriage patterns in both areas. In the west region generally, farms are smaller, incomes lower, and a higher proportion of farm operators are unmarried. In short the region exhibits the characteristics which Hannan (1979) associates with the dissolution of a peasant economy. This is quite different from the more prosperous east where a higher proportion of farms hold out a better opportunity of material well-being. We would expect these differences then to be reflected in the marriage circumstances of the farm women in the present study.

The Women Who Became Farm Wives

The fact that so many women left rural Ireland suggests that apart from the non-availability of employment locally, there was a kind of consensus among them as to the undesirability of the life of a farm wife in which subordination was obvious and work was so harsh. Those who did become farm wives are somewhat exceptional in that they became involved in farming when few of their sisters would have done so. This is particularly the case in the west where distaste for life on the small farms there was such that most farm daughters left rural areas as soon as they could. In the east on the other hand, where farming was generally more prosperous, marriage to a farmer did not appear to be such an undesirable prospect, provided the holding size afforded the probability of a decent standard of living. We would expect therefore the life histories and accounts of the circumstances of marriage of women in the two areas to be quite different.

Farm Wives' Origins and Education

In the west, the wives of farmers come overwhelmingly from farming backgrounds. All but two (who were from the local area) had been raised on farms, usually less than ten miles from their present homes. They had in most cases an intimate knowledge of the culture and conditions which they would face after marriage. In the east, however, 37 percent (11/30) of the women interviewed came from non-farming backgrounds and of these, seven came from outside the locality, from non-rural areas ranging from city to small town. Regional differences were also very evident in the women's levels of education, the west again showing a distinctly different pattern. In the west, 37 percent (11/30) had primary education only, with all but one of these women aged over fifty. In the east however there was just one woman with primary education only. Of those who had second level education, a similar proportion in the west (42 percent) and east (38 percent) had dropped out after two to three years, leaving school at age fourteen or fifteen, or after completing the Intermediate Certificate. Five women in the west and eight in the east had completed secondary education and obtained the Leaving Certificate and an additional six western women and ten from the east had professional training (such as nursing) or a university degree.

The most striking aspect of the farm wives' educational attainment is the relatively high proportion of those in the west who had no secondary schooling. This is also evident from the wider survey[2] where 41 percent of western farm wives had primary education only, compared to 21 percent in the east. Although the eastern women have a slightly younger age profile, the extent of these differences cannot be explained by age. Only two of the 15 women aged over fifty in the west had post primary education, compared to all 13 in the same age category in the east, with five of the latter having completed Leaving Certificate or higher. Among younger women the differences are not so stark, the corresponding figures being 63 percent for the west and 78 percent for the east, for those aged under forty. One would expect of course a lower level of educational attainment for older women, as participation rates generally have risen considerably over the past few decades. Women aged over fifty at the time of the study would have been entering second level education during the late 1940s and early 1950s, long before the introduction of 'free' post-primary education in 1967, whereas those now under forty would have been entering second level during the 1960s and 1970s. A previous study of educational participation among farm children in the west of Ireland had shown that among daughters who entered the labour force during the period from 1937 to 1951, 32 percent had some post-primary education. In the period from 1952 to 1966 the proportion rose to 69 percent and from 1967 onwards it rose to 95 percent (Conway and O'Hara, 1986: 259). Daughters' participation was much higher than that of sons. Hannan's (1970) study of young people in a western

2. This wider survey from which the sixty farms in the present study were selected is described in detail in Chapter Three.

county also revealed a high level of participation among farm daughters, which was again much higher than that of sons. When participation was related to the farm valuation (a measure of the productive capacity of the farm), even at the lowest levels four-fifths of females had some post-primary education.

In both these studies, the higher participation of daughters was interpreted in terms of parents (and, presumably daughters themselves) attempting to enhance their occupational prospects outside their own areas where job opportunities were likely to be less limited. (It will be remembered from the previous section that these gender differences in educational participation began in the nineteenth century). This interpretation is confirmed by a further study of west of Ireland women (O'Hara, 1987b) which captured the migration effect, by focusing on the occupational patterns of cohorts and distinguishing by decade of first entry to the labour force. More than forty percent of these women who began their working life in the 1950s were found to be resident outside Ireland and a further eleven percent in Dublin. Of those who entered in successive decades up to the 1980s, less than a quarter resided within ten miles of their original home. Marriage rates were much lower among women who migrated and single women were more skilled and better educated (O'Hara, 1987b: 80–81). It appears then that in the west, migration is strongly associated with educational attainment so that the women who remained in the area and married farmers were generally those with lower levels of education.

Regrettably we do not have similar information for farm daughters from the east, but the higher attainment levels of eastern women in the present study reflect the differences in class composition and socio-economic profile of the two areas. Sixty percent of these women had completed secondary schooling or higher, compared to 37 percent in the west. This was also evident in the wider survey where the corresponding proportions were 52 percent and 39 percent. In this context it should be remembered that more than a third of the respondents in the east were not themselves farm daughters, whereas in the west only two of the respondents were not raised on farms.

Occupational Comparisons

The educational differences just discussed are reflected in the pre-marriage occupations of the farm women as shown in Table 4.1.

Two-thirds of the women in the east compared to less than half of those in the west came from white-collar occupations. Twice as many in the west were in manufacturing and service type work and an equal

Table 4.1
Pre-Marriage Occupational Categories of Respondents

| | West | | East | |
Occupational Category	%	No.	%	No.
Professional	20	6	33	10
Clerical	27	8	33	10
Manufacturing	17	5	3	1
Sales and Service	23	7	17	5
At home	13	4	13	4
Total	100	30	100	30

number of women in each area had remained at home until marriage. These comparisons reflect the class differences between the two regions – the occupations of farm wives in the east having a more middle-class character in line with the characteristics of the farming structure there and the considerable proportion of them from non-farming backgrounds. Farm wives in the west on the other hand, themselves raised on small holdings, were mainly engaged in lower paid factory, service, and clerical work before marriage. In several cases, they had also emigrated – eight women from the west worked in Britain or the United States prior to marriage, five of these had no post primary education and the remaining three had no more than three years.

Farm women in the west who had low levels of education and poorly paid low-status jobs may have had a more restricted choice in terms of career options or marriage partners than their better educated siblings and the majority of the women in the east. They were in effect the ones who stayed in, or returned to, the locality when the general tendency for women was to escape. In this sense they can be seen as being at the bottom of a family hierarchy of material resources where inheriting sons are at the top, followed by non-inheriting siblings with non-farm occupations. Marriage to a farmer may have presented a more desirable option than their limited occupational choices, as well as offering those who wished to return home an opportunity to do so. From their own perspective, they would have had to give up relatively little in income terms and would have gained the status of being married as well as the opportunity to become mothers. However, material explanations of this kind run the risk of over-simplifying the complexity of issues involved. As we shall see in the following sections, and more particularly when we come to examine women's work in the next chapter, these women's willingness to marry into farming (unlike most of their sisters), and their familiarity with the culture and life-style of family farming, gave some of them room to negotiate a marital relationship in which they manage to significantly challenge and erode patriarchal structures. Farm women in the east on the other hand came to the family farm from predominantly white-collar occupations. More than a third came from non-farming backgrounds and 23 percent from outside the locality. They are a more diverse category than those in the west and 37 percent of them continue to either work in paid employment (full-time and part-time) or run their own businesses compared to 20 percent in the west.

The Circumstances of Marriage

The clear educational and occupational differences in the backgrounds of farm wives suggest considerable variation in the circumstances of marriage and distinct differences between west and east. Moreover, the age range of the women in the study means that their marriages were contracted over four decades. In the west, the earliest marriage occurred in 1952 and the most recent in 1984. In the east, the time span involved is from 1951 to 1989. The fact that the period over which these women married extends to almost forty years provides an opportunity to construct a long-term perspective on the changes in the circumstances in which women marry farmers and the shifts in expectations and understanding of what the marriage contract involves. It is evident that women married in quite different contexts across time and space and that their pre-marriage status left many of them little 'cultural capital' to bring to the marriage (Bourdieu, 1977). Moreover, while the majority of women married into farming, in the sense that their husbands were farming at the time of marriage, this is not the case for all the women in the study. In three instances in the west it was the wives who had been the only available successors to their fathers' farms as there were no sons in the families concerned. In two of these the husband 'married in' to the wife's family farm and in the other the couple met and married abroad, returning later to farm the wife's family holding and take care of her ageing mother. Three couples in the west married abroad before returning to take over the husband's family holding.

In the east, there was one case where the couple purchased a farm after marriage, two cases of husbands 'marrying in' and one other where the wife's father had purchased a farm for her after her marriage. The particularities of these situations will be referred to in later chapters, but it is important to note that they are exceptions and that in all cases where women inherited farms it was as a result of the absence of an appropriate male successor or, in one case, a (wealthy) father's benevolence to his daughter. The significance of marriage to a farmer is also influenced by the importance of farming to the couples' livelihood. If husbands have another occupation, farming may be perceived as a secondary activity with which women have little identification or active involvement. On the other hand, where farming is an important source of income for the family, the event of their husbands' taking up off-farm work may plunge women into a farm-work role which they had not anticipated.

We now turn to the women's accounts of the circumstances of their marriages. These tell us much about their sense of control over their lives, the choices they felt were available to them, and the consequences of their choices. They also reveal the strength of cultural and ideological influences and how these differ between east and west. In the first analysis, the material is organised around two particular situations because they provide striking illustrations of these processes: the case of women who married directly from home (without taking up work outside their home farms); and those who emigrated but subsequently returned to Ireland to life as a farm wife.

Marrying from Home

There were four women (13 percent) in each area who had 'stayed at home' before marriage. For them, becoming a wife provided a status and security which was seen as almost inevitable – the remnants of an older system in which unmarried daughters remained at home until a suitable match could be found. Although none of these women admitted to a 'match' and most were quite forthright about the circumstances in which they met and courted their husbands, they entered marriage in a different context from women who had been in waged work. They had stayed at home because of family obligations, or because their educational attainments did not allow them to get a job of sufficient status, but it was taken for granted that they would eventually marry and their staying at home to help was seen as a temporary state:

> I was raised on a farm and nursing people. My mother died when I was seven and I nursed my father and uncle. I never went to secondary school or had a job. I don't regret it, my father was very good. When I married here my father-in-law was here and after thirteen years he got a stroke and I nursed him too. Nowadays young people won't live with their in-laws and they are right. It's not fair to the older generation, they have a different view, espe-

cially about rearing kids. We'll be the same ourselves, I suppose. I'd hope that neither of my daughters would marry a farmer. It is a struggle and that's it. They say they won't be tied to the kitchen sink. (W4, aged 59)

For such a woman, marriage brought a continuation of a caring role hitherto enacted on her home farm and she is conscious of being part of an established system of expectations and responsibilities, typical of the west of Ireland, but no longer acceptable to the younger generation. Such women are keenly aware of being the ones who stayed at home and opted for a life of 'hardship', while others fled rural Ireland:

> I was happy to leave home and I got married at twenty three. I left secondary school after one year; there were lots of jobs in the shops but my mother said: 'stay at home and we will fortune you'. So I did. Maybe if I had been working I might have felt differently but in farming you are your own boss. . . My sisters wouldn't marry a farmer. They went to America and once they got the taste of it they wouldn't come back. I suppose my mother's hard life put them off, they didn't want a life of misery in farming. (W7, aged 51)

> There were just two sisters [in my family] and we did a lot of farm work. . . I left school at fifteen. I was never trained. Others went to England and did well enough even though they didn't have much training or education. I really regret this. (W24, aged 63)

These accounts from the west are not unexpected; they are the somewhat rueful reflections of women who stayed behind and who are conscious of being part of the remnants of a now obsolete system of family obligations. They knew what was expected of them, viz. the creation of a new farm family with attendant responsibilities for domestic work, farm work, childbearing and rearing – in short, acceptance of a totality of work roles and priorities defined by the needs of the family farm. The extent to which they would be able to challenge the subordination associated with such a status would depend in large part on the kind of conjugal contract which evolved between wife and husband and their own definition of their commitment to the family enterprise. This will become clear in the next chapter when we look at the work roles of farm women but it is worth mentioning here that, of the two women quoted immediately above, the first expressed a great deal of satisfaction with her life in farming and had a considerable influence on the farming enterprise, whereas the second expressed an acute sense of subordination, almost of entrapment.

Women in the east, who had married from home, talked of this more in terms of regret at the loss of vocational and occupational opportunities and the limited options available to them. They are also conscious of how unacceptable such limited choices would be to the younger generation:

> I left school after the Inter. Cert. [Intermediate Certificate] and I have always regretted it. . . I stayed with my mother until I got married. If I had done the Leaving [Certificate] I probably would have gone on for nursing but my mother was not well. . . My daughters' lives will be very different to mine. (E10, aged 45)

> I married at twenty. . . I deeply regret the fact that I never worked, never had a wage. I stayed at home. One of my sisters got married and my mother said: 'you'll stay at home'. I never had a wage. . . I'd love to be young nowadays, there is great freedom. (E25, aged 53)

> I went to secondary school for three years. I would have liked to stay longer but I was needed at home, the younger ones had that opportunity. I stayed at home until I was married at age twenty three. (E7, aged 50)

The only woman from the east not to have second level education also married from home, but in a quite different context:

> I was the second eldest, and my older brother stayed at home at thirteen to help out. Then he got TB so I was next in line. I left school at thirteen, never went beyond national school. . . I came home and stayed with my father and got down to business. I was the main farmer with him and I loved it. I worked at home until I was twenty two, then I got married. My mother-in-law, father-in-law and husband's brother were here. The brother was only here for a year and a half. It wasn't really a problem. I was working out on the farm and the mother was very independent and worked in the house. That was fine with me. (E23, aged 47)

There is less of a sense of inevitability perhaps in these accounts than in those of the western women, less of a sense of the weight of culture which is also very strong in the stories of those who returned home to farm.

Returning from Abroad

The regional differences in emigration experience are very apparent. Eight women in the west but only two[3] in the east had worked abroad (in the United States or Britain) and returned to be farm wives in Ireland. This happened in two ways: either the woman, having worked

---

3. One of these had moved from the west to the east through a Land Commission resettlement scheme several years after marriage. The other woman in the east spent less than two years in the United States.

abroad for some years, returned to marry a local farmer whom she may have met before emigrating or on a home visit; or the couple met and married abroad and then returned to take over the farm:

> I was in America for six years before I got married. I worked in a shop here first and then went over to my sister. . . I came home on holidays and met my husband. I then came home to marry two years later. My sister followed in time and is married here now. (W5, aged 57)

> I was in England for ten to twelve years. . . I then went to New York. I had been working with an American family in England and they sponsored me to go to America. I had a sister in New York and I stayed there for five years. I came home and met my husband at an ordination, I promised him I'd come back and I did. . . Of course I found it difficult when I came home, going on a bicycle, carrying shopping and so on. (W11, aged 68)

For the couples who married abroad, the decision to return was usually the husband's with the desire for farming and/or the sense of family obligation as the primary motivation. The women feel that they had few real options, other than presumably outright refusal. However, their ties of affection and loyalty and the children's welfare were the most frequent reasons offered for the decision, however unwilling, to move back to Ireland. In the one case, in the west, where after eleven years of marriage in England the family returned to a farm which the wife had inherited, the woman concerned indicated that a sense of obligation to her widowed mother dictated the decision.

For the farm wife, returning to farm in the west of Ireland usually meant a drastic drop in living standards and often having to share living accommodation with her in-laws:

> I hated coming back [from England] but I did it for his sake. I thought it would be better for the kids who were four and two at the time. We lived with his mother at first and it was difficult. You had no privacy and it was an old house with no central heating. We had our own house in London. . . Our standard of living was better in England, we had a phone twenty years ago and we have no phone here now. . . It's nice for the kids being in Ireland, being home, I'm still not sorry that we did it. (W2, aged 50)

> I would have preferred to stay [in England] but never said so as I didn't want to influence him and he was thinking of his father and mother. So we came back and brought a lot of our stuff and for the first few months we lived with my mother. We had our own house in England and there was no water here and I had an eight-month-old colicky baby. I muddled on from one day to another and it was always dark and wet when you looked outside. I got fed up so many times. (W28, aged 66)

> I was reared on a farm and never liked it. I saw my mother slaving and said this is not for me and yet I ended up here. I thought I'd have longer before coming back to the farm from England but my husband talked me into it. There was nothing else in my husband's life only farming. . . We had to start from nothing, the place was a wilderness with the old house, two rooms and a kitchen, no electricity, no water, no tongs even which was very important in those days. (W25, aged 60)

The strong sense of obligation and constraint which comes from these comments reveal the women's understanding and acceptance of the kinship commitments associated with family farming. It is not hard to imagine that husbands may have felt similarly about the obligations of kinship which brought them back to a farm in the west of Ireland, and a substantial drop in standard of living. It is a measure of the strength of the commitment to family continuity in family farming that it could extend its influence to emigrants in this way.

Early Marriage – Mothers and In-laws

Whatever a woman's pre-marriage status, marriage to a farmer usually means entry to a farm which has been controlled by his family. She enters a family system with sets of values, norms and practices which are well established before her arrival. Among the older women in the study this commonly meant shared residence with the husband's family, particularly in the west. But these women, and younger women from farming backgrounds, were entering a familiar situation. They had watched their own mothers in the role of farm wife. While their sisters may have migrated through a wish to escape from what they perceived as the drudgery of their mothers' lives, the mother is a constant referent for daughters who become farm wives, particularly in the west. Many western women were working on the home farm from early childhood and compare their own lives to their mothers' with a sense of awe at their fortitude and a sense of relief at the improvements which have lessened the burdens for themselves:

> I was raised on a farm and did everything on the farm. My sister did the housework. I was thinning beet which is hard work but I didn't mind it. You felt you had to help out. I worked on the bog too and picking potatoes. There were four in the family and all are in Ireland. Looking back now I think my mother had a hard life – peeling potatoes and boiling big pots for pigs and drawing water. (W5, aged 57)

> My mother worked in the fields. She had eighteen children and was deprived of a lot. . . She had a baby in a cradle and used to leave it with the old man [her father-in-law] while she went out and worked. There is no work now compared to that. People complain today but they don't understand what people like her had to do. (W7, aged 51)

> Mother had twelve children and two old people to look after as well. She had no real freedom, her whole life was about caring for others. . . The main difference between her life and mine is that I must go out on a Saturday night. (W15, aged 34)

> There were sixteen in the family on forty acres. Seven or eight of them are now outside Ireland. My mother didn't believe in birth control and did all the outside work because my father was working [off the farm]. I didn't wonder at farming because I was brought up with it. My sisters in England think I'm mad. (W16, aged 40)

None of the women from the east described their mother's lives in these terms. Although some of their mothers did carry out physical work on the farm, it was not as common and was never described in the same arduous terms as the work of farm women in the west. Moreover, mothers in the east were much more likely to have had paid help:

> My mother looked after the garden and the orchard, the vegetables and flowers. She had hens and ducks and geese but not anymore. (E14, aged 28)

> Times were hard for my mother but she had plenty of help. She didn't drive of course like women today but now women have more pressure running the kids here and there. . . The main difference between me and my mother was that I could drive, I had that freedom, I could get out. She must have been bored but she lived for her children and she always had company. (E25, aged 53)

The more commercialised and prosperous farming in the east was reflected in the lives of the mothers of the women there. While many saw their mother's subordinate status in terms of having had 'less freedom' or fewer conveniences than they themselves have, their experience of growing up on a farm did not encompass the harsh physical privation common in the west. They were however, conscious of the constraints that cultural prescriptions and religious ideology imposed on their mothers:

> My mother would never go out on her own. My parents didn't drink and they didn't socialise. . . I think husbands now understand women better. My husband would help more. My father didn't understand women, he got on fine with my mother but they were more friends, better friends than anything. (E14, aged 28)

They had it harder, having children every year and not having automatic washing machines or dishwashers. They didn't go out to work after they got married, they got pregnant and if they didn't after a year or two, questions were being asked. I get on great with my mother, especially since I got married and had children myself. I think their religion was taken too seriously especially from the point of view of having children. (E21, aged 30)

The constraints which these women articulate are not however particular to farm women. The restrictions of farming are not what they remember about their mothers' lives but rather the confinements of culture and ideology by which the lives of all women were circumscribed. Those who come from non-farming backgrounds have no real farming reference and often bring with them the culture of a more structured and materialistic way of life which contrasts sharply with what they find in farm and country life:

Town people are more geared to women working, regular hours and shopping. People in the country do with less in terms of social life, housing, and clothes – sometimes too little. There is a happy medium. Most of the time I am contented here but holidays are not part of their way of life. They take no holidays, they don't mind muck and dirt and go around with their hair not washed. If you keep on working in the home there is no need to go to the trouble. If you go out you have to take a personal interest. (E17, aged 32)

For others there is the shock of realising that farming is actually a family business involving two generations and a range of taken-for-granted family obligations:

I never really thought at all about farming. If I knew then what I know now I might have seen it differently. What I mean is that we are supporting two households. I was not aware of this, I just didn't know. It was not inconsiderate on H's[4] part not to tell me, he was just used to the situation. (E29, aged 46)

For older women in the west on the other hand, family obligation was part of the marriage arrangement. Sharing accommodation with the husband's family was usual. These women frequently recall their in-laws with affection and acknowledge that their help and moral support was important in the early days of marriage. Their strong identification with their own mothers probably helped ease potential tensions with mothers-in-law. Moreover, several women in the west mentioned the importance of the in-laws' pensions as a contribution to the family income:

4. 'H', as mentioned in Chapter Three, is used for respondents' references to their husbands throughout the book.

When I got married I moved into the old house here in 1962. It was thatched with no facilities and my father and mother-in-law were here. I got on very well with them. She was only fifty nine when I came in here and died only seven years ago. He died in 1971, he had arthritis and was in a wheelchair. . . My mother-in-law taught me to milk. She gave me the easy cows. My husband was working [off the farm] at the time. She helped on the farm and looked after my father-in-law. (W5, aged 57)

I moved in here with my parents-in-law and they both lived to be very old. They were here for twenty two years. I got on very well with them. I was nervous at first; people said to me hadn't I great courage but my mother-in-law was a great help when the babies came. She even insisted that I go to [a private] hospital to have my first baby so that I would be treated well. (W7, aged 51)

However, western women stress that these situations are no longer acceptable and that young couples nowadays need privacy to be able to establish a space for themselves, separate from the older generation:

This is my husband's home place and his parents were here when we married. It worked out well. I wasn't nervous about moving in really, granddad is still here but he has his room and TV. . . Two women in one kitchen doesn't really work out. Being together seven days a week is difficult, you need space but there is no problem if you have room – this is a big house so there is plenty of room. Some women won't give up their freedom and move in with the in-laws so many young people are building their own homes these days. (W30, aged 36)

When we got married, his mother and father were here and we built on to the house. Separate apartments in the house was a good idea. I don't think any two women should be in one kitchen, it's not fair to them. . . What we did at the time was a new thing, I wish we had the guts to build our own house. The hardest thing is the lack of privacy. The older women didn't mind that. (W6, aged 46)

When my son and his wife were getting married, they had to build a house. I suggested they might like to move in here, after all she would be out working all day. But they would have none of it. People want their own home now. (W3, aged 59)

Building a new house or providing a separate apartment for the husband's parents is seen as the most appropriate solution to the need for new couples to establish a separate identity and it is the women who usually insist on this. Sharing the family farm may be unavoidable but younger women in the west are clear about the need to create a separate farm family home:

When I married I lived with my mother-in-law for eighteen months but I made sure the house was started before we married. I wanted my own key, my own house with my own things. We moved in here a few months before N was born. . . H was keen to stay but I didn't want everyone telling me what to do. (W14, aged 32)

In the east this resistance to incorporation into the husband's family system is even more marked and longer established:

The house was built when we married so we had no in-laws. It is very difficult for some people but it often works out well. Now a lot are putting in granny flats and I think that is a great idea. When you have separate apartments each has his own. (E10, aged 45)

We began building the house before we were married and lived in a mobile home until it was ready. We moved in after our first baby was born and it was just a shell but I wouldn't live with my in-laws. (E8, aged 32)

We lived for a month in a rented house. I wouldn't live with my in-laws, I'd prefer a place of my own. You can do your own thing, get up when you like. You can do what you like in your own house. (E14, aged 28)

When we were married I wouldn't move in [with husband's family] even though it was discussed. You would need privacy and independence, you couldn't have a row. We are close enough [to them] as it is but we have no problems. (E17, aged 32)

This insistence on the establishment of a separate home, and independence from family control, reflects a shift already well established in the east towards increased 'nucleation' of farm families as well as an ideology of separateness and of the need for privacy. Among younger women this is linked to an aspiration for a different kind of marital relationship involving the idea of autonomy for the couple and sharing within the marriage, whereby the husband's behaviour is expected to be different from that of his (or her own) father:

The old people had certain ideas about what to do. For instance my mother-in-law was here one day and I said something about H getting his own dinner and I could see she was shocked. . . Men are changing too, H is not the same as his father. In his house the women did the running for the men. The men worked and the women took care of them. That is all changing and farmers are more outgoing. If I suggest holidays to H he says we'll go. The old people had their own ways and that was it. (E3, aged 36)

The family revolved around the father before, now it revolves around the children. Men are changing . . . women have changed the men, they are not putting up with as much, not prepared to be servants any more. . . We were always told, don't make noise, you'll disturb your father. Children were to be seen and not heard. Even though he brought us places on Sundays and all that and was very good, he was the man of the house. (E21, aged 30)

These changing ideologies constitute an important reason for younger women to remain in, or return to, paid work after marriage in order to maintain a sense of financial independence and the family's standard of living. This can also be a way of asserting the farm wife's independence and distancing herself from the farm operation. As one younger woman from a non-farming background in the east put it 'it's the man, not the farm that you marry'. The majority of the women in the study areas however did 'marry the farm' in the sense of not retaining a separate - vocational identity or independent source of income after marriage, and becoming more or less incorporated into the farm as a family business. This is generally the case in the west where all but six farm wives are not working outside the farm or home and is also prevalent in the east, where more than half (19/30), usually the older women, are in the same situation.

These women have a strong consciousness of the subordination associated with women's incorporation into the family farm and how it is sustained by ideologies of marriage and 'wifehood'. Their own experience of powerlessness, regarding, for instance, the size of their families, or their lack of freedom and independence particularly in the early years of their marriage, is allied to a sense of being part of a wider set of structures and ideologies which define the terms of their existence. The fact that these ideologies are changing, and that farm wives' material dependence on their husbands can be lessened by engaging in paid work, are perceived by the older women as reducing farm women's subordination. They see marriage into farming as altogether different for modern women who are gradually being freed from many of the strictures which constrained themselves:

Everything has changed – going out to work, having fewer children, keeping on their jobs after marriage, having a social life as well as the men, becoming more equal. I think it is a good thing. (W5, aged 57)

Women are now talking more, they were very quiet and in the background in the past. . . Many got married straight from school and had no experience of anything outside. One of my sisters-in-law wouldn't go anywhere without her husband. (W3, aged 59)

Women nowadays have their own independence, their own money to fall back on and money for the house. I wouldn't like to be without any of my family [seven children] but life then consisted of muddling through days and washing nappies. I'd go along with the present trend to space and limit the family. (W28, aged 66)

There is more sharing nowadays among women and men. There were so many bachelors in the past because there was no such thing as two homes on the farm. The girls went, they didn't want pure slavery. Men were really pampered in the past and the work of women taken for granted. (W25, aged 60)

Women have more independence, they don't have to work as hard in the fields, with cows and hens and chickens and rear children at the same time, it is much easier for my daughters. (W23, aged 51)

Modern women let the men know how they feel, it's fifty-fifty all the time. They make them [the men] share in everything and let them know how they feel. We were brought up to feel that the woman was the heart of the home and that it was her job to keep him happy. It's only fair for women, why should we be slaves. (E13, aged 51)

Women in my day didn't think like they do now – we only went out to the ICA [Irish Countrywomen's Association]. I suppose we were tired and bored but we got through. The winters were tough and every summer I would be pregnant. (E25, aged 53)

Women were kept down – they accepted everything. . . No, I wouldn't do the same again, I wouldn't accept everything. I would question everything. (E24, aged 51)

Younger women, on the other hand, have been able to enter marriage in a stronger position by bringing human capital assets to the marriage in the form of professional training or marketable skills. By working in paid employment or running their own businesses such women have been able to challenge the traditional position of the farm wife in the power structure of the farm family. They are quite clear about what differentiates them from the older generation of farm wives. As one young farm wife put it:

There is now a new generation of farm women. Women married farmers in the past to be a farmer's wife. That doesn't happen any more. Most of the young women have jobs and work for money, although I'm sure most get job satisfaction too. . . I don't know what would make me give up work now. I can't think of anything that would; I'd hate to be at home all day. (W14, aged 32)

Whether working outside the home actually lessens or merely changes the character of farm women's subordination will become clearer in later chapters. However, women themselves see it as a way of ensuring a more independent role for themselves, and consider the generation of an independent income an important means of lessening their subordination and enhancing their power within the domestic situation. Whether they actually have that option depends on their pre-marriage skills, local labour market conditions, and the attitude of their husbands. The majority of farm women do not have an off-farm income and have therefore to employ different strategies to contest the patriarchal structures in which they are embedded.

Reflections and Implications

In this chapter we have seen that migration of women from rural Ireland and their reluctance to remain in family farming can be interpreted as a form of resistance to the patriarchal structures and hard physical labour of Irish family farming, particularly on smaller holdings. This has had a profound effect on the demographic and social structure of rural Ireland. Ironically, the stem family system, which had been established to maintain the continuity of family farming through ensuring the transfer of patrimony intact to one male heir, had the ultimate effect of disrupting continuity because this same heir often encountered difficulty in finding a wife. This happened earlier, and in a different way, in the east where class difference (as reflected in size of farm) was the primary determinant of farmers' ability to attract a marriage partner. It appears that farmers on larger holdings in the more commercialised farming areas had less difficulty in finding a wife, but we know far less about the dynamics of marriage among this farming class because most of the research has been focused on the west where smallholders predominated. In his study of rural social change Hannan (1979) associated falling marriage rates among farmers in the post-war period with the disintegration of a 'peasant' farming economy, with its own distinctive culture, in the west of Ireland. However, neither Hannan's work nor any other study addresses the social processes in the east in the same way, and so accounts of demographic and social processes there are, of necessity, more speculative. (This was an important reason for including both west and east in the present study).

In the earlier part of this chapter, the analysis of demographic trends and previous studies may appear to have propelled the discussion too far into an east/west differentiation. However, the personal accounts of the life histories and marriage circumstances of the women interviewed have uncovered major differences in the social and cultural context between west and east. The women's accounts throw into sharp relief their own understanding of the very limited choices available to them. Those who married from home articulate the sense of inevitability and absence of vocational choice which determined the fate of so many farm wives in the past. Those who returned from abroad were often caught in the web of family obligations, cultural values and ideologies of wifehood which prompted their return to Ireland even at the expense of a substantial drop in living standards. In their accounts of their early married life, women in the west described harsh and (by modern standards) uncomfortable lives, tempered by memories of their mothers' even more rigorous life histories. Poor material circumstances and their sense of the weight of culture, ideology and family obligations distinguished them from women in the east who had fewer experiences of privation and appeared for various reasons, including their more diverse backgrounds, to distance themselves more from the family farm.

Yet despite the harshness of the early married lives of women in the west, and their consciousness of the structures which constrained them, their accounts suggest a vigour and strength which challenges any view of farm wives as powerless victims of structure and culture. In their descriptions of the early days of marriage there is much evidence of creative adjustment to constraints which need not always be seen only in negative terms, such as the presence of in-laws. Moreover in a situation where few young women were aspiring to become farm wives, they may have been admired and cherished by their husbands and their husbands' families for their willingness to take on what so many had avoided, thus giving them some leverage to contest and negotiate patriarchal structures.

It is apparent that those who bring 'cultural capital' to the marriage in the form of professional training generally continue to retain their pre-marriage occupation, and that this has implications for the labour process and for power relations within the farm family. Having an independent income is regarded by younger women as an important source of independence and autonomy in marriage, and this issue will emerge as critical to women's position within farm and family in the chapters which follow. The older women interviewed are painfully aware of the restrictions and missed opportunities in their own lives and they perceive ideologies of marriage and family which stress sharing, privacy and financial independence for women as freeing contemporary farm wives from some of the constraints which they themselves encountered. They see themselves as the last generation who were willing to accede to such an extent to the demands of family and farm. Younger farm women articulate these changes and bring different expectations to marriage and family which stress 'modern' values, and include a new home and a desire for a higher material standard of living.

Despite the significance of regional differences in much of the discussion so far, and the apparent influence of distinct cultures associated with different farming circumstances in setting the broad parameters of farm women's lives, it would be misleading to imply that cultural influences are determinate. More proximate intra-farm family factors may be shown to be much more significant as we move further inside the family farm. In Chapter Five we attempt to investigate how women confront the patriarchal structures of family farming in day-to-day life by focusing on the work that they do both on and off the family farm.

5

INSIDE THE FAMILY FARM

Women's Work and Family Farming

Introduction

The analysis and discussion in the previous chapter confirmed that the establishment of farm families through marriage is associated with a range of mixes of material circumstances, cultural conditions, and ideologies which influence the evolution of gender relations within farm families. It was clearly established that farm women's subordination has evoked strategies of resistance and negotiation which challenge ideas of determinism or of women as passive victims, and imply that women's own definition of their working lives as well as intra-family dynamics may be important in understanding their status. We have already suggested some sources of farm women's empowerment, such as the 'cultural capital' they bring to the marriage and, not least their scarcity value, and hence the negotiating leverage of those willing to become farm wives in the first place. To explore these issues further, we turn in this chapter to the heart of family farming, to the labour process, that is the work that women do on the family farm and their working relationships. We wish to establish the nature and extent of their work role(s); how the gendered organisation of work subordinates women; and finally, the ways in which patriarchal power relations are contested and negotiated through working relationships. We will also consider women's off-farm work in terms of its significance for the family farm and for farm wives empowerment.

Attempts to understand the nature and meaning of women's work on farms, immediately run into conceptual difficulties. What is to be defined as work? Conventional studies of the gender division of labour on farms tend to confine themselves to a fairly narrow definition of family labour, usually documenting women's non-domestic work as it relates to the farm enterprise, that is their involvement in farm tasks and decision making (Jones and Rosenfeld, 1981; Buchanan et al., 1982; Sheridan, 1982; Reimer, 1986; Gasson, 1992; Keating and Little, 1994; Alston, 1995). But women are involved in farm work in a family context and, unless they have another vocational role off the farm, it is their work as farm wives which gives them an occupational identity and can provide personal fulfilment. The work of a farm wife usually involves household work and childcare in addition to any farm work, so studies which focus only on women's work for the market obscure their work in the farm family. As Delphy and Leonard have argued, such work is invisible precisely because it occurs within the family context (1992: 93).

It is important therefore to include in the analysis all the work that women do, shifting the focus from the work itself to the person doing the work. The starting point is not then, the 'labour requirements' of the family farm, and how women 'fit in' to these, but rather the actual work of women on different kinds of family farms, both on the farm itself, in the household and off the farm, all of which can be for the family farm, directly or indirectly contributing to its maintenance. The different work circumstances can be seen as separate spheres of activity, which occur within the context of the farm family, because regardless of whether or not she carries out 'farm work', the farm wife is working for the farm family. Before turning to consideration of women's activities inside the family farm, we look first at the way in which the work of women on farms and in other family enterprises is ignored or devalued in the public arena.

Farm Wives' Official Invisibility

The tendency to disregard all of women's work which is outside the waged marketplace, or to regard it as not 'productive', underpins the phenomenon of farm wives' invisibility in official statistics. The family farm as an entity, or the farmer as an occupational category, are commonly the basic units of analysis in agrarian studies and statistics on agriculture. Insofar as individual family or household members are considered, it is within the context of the labour or decision-making requirements of the farm business. Even though such studies (often through questions addressed to the male farmer) have found that farm wives are engaged in work which is directly contributing to the generation of an income for the farm family, this has not led to any occupational recognition for farm women. The occupational classifications associated with farming in Ireland are: 'the farmer' taken to mean the registered holder of the land; and 'relatives assisting' designed to include family members, other than the farm wife, who may be working on the farm. Since farm women are in the first place wives, and any farm work that they do is regarded as unpaid, they are relegated to the category 'housewives'. Thus begins a tautology allowing the work that women do on farms to be ignored since women themselves are not categorised as farm workers. The work that men do becomes synonymous with farm work and since women's work is not farm work (and has no recognised monetary value), it is therefore not important and farm wives can be dismissed as unimportant (Hill, 1980: 373).

Treatment of the farm in a unitary way so that usually only one occupation, that of the farm operator, and one income, that of the family, is associated with it, is the convention in Irish national agricultural statistics and in the yearly National Farm Surveys carried out by Teagasc.[1] The farm is the unit of analysis, so that the main classifications associated with these surveys are based on the farm (e.g., output, costs, income). The labour inputs of individual members of the farm family are not published in these surveys, and until recently the male was taken to be the farm operator except in a small minority of cases (6 percent in 1990) where a woman was so classified. In more recent surveys, farm operators are not classified by gender in the published reports (see Teagasc, 1991; Power and Roche, 1995). The association of farm operator with the male extends even to cases where the husband has another occupation, because the landowner is deemed to be the farmer. It also probably reflects the normative association of farmer with male on the part of those collecting the information and on the part of farm families themselves. For instance when the (all male) recorders collected data for the wider survey from the households included in the present study,[2] they classified the male as the farm operator even in situations where the woman was the sole or co-owner of the land and was clearly running the farm. The association of farm with male is so culturally embedded that a woman is only seen as the farmer in those situations where there is no possibility of so classifying a male.

As was pointed out in Chapter One, women on farms were included for the first time in the 1991 Census of Agriculture (Central Statistics

1. Teagasc is the national body which is responsible for advice, research, education and training services to the agriculture and food industry

2. These interviews were carried out for the wider survey with which the present study is associated. This is described in Chapter Three.

Office, 1994b) if they were involved in 'farm work'. According to this Census there were 91,400 female family members on family farms in Ireland. Of these, more than two-thirds (70 percent) were the spouses of the farm holder. Even figures such as these usually under-represent women's contribution to the farm, as the definition of work on which they are based is often restricted to manual and the more visible managerial tasks such as book-keeping and accounting. Furthermore, a range of tasks associated with the farm business – from running errands, to dealing with callers, to involvement in farm decisions – are not defined as farm work. This is a common problem in labour statistics across the world (Boulding, 1980; Waring, 1988; Fahey, 1990). Within the European Union there are no accurate published accounts of women's involvement in farming in the Member States, either in terms of the numbers involved or the nature of their contribution to family farming. Indeed the extent to which women are marginalised in the vast array of statistics on European farming is such that there is far more information available on the animals and crops on family farms than on the women.

Consequently, women's work on family farms is largely invisible in the public domain of labour and agricultural statistics. Farm women generally are not considered as farmers, and are officially ignored in an industry which is publicly controlled by men through male-dominated farming organisations and agribusiness. Women have internalised this definition of their occupational status so that in self-classificatory surveys such as the Census of Population, farm women classify themselves as housewives. For instance, in the 1991 Census of Agriculture (which, unlike the Census of Population, is not a self-completion survey) 16,400 women were categorised as farm holders but this is 9,600 more than classified themselves as such in the Census of Population for the same year. Apart from those women who had a clearly recognised occupation in the paid labour force, all of the women in the present study categorised themselves as 'housewives' in the 1991 Census, usually explaining this by saying that they never thought of putting down anything else.

In the remainder of this chapter we look first at Arensberg and Kimball's (1968) description of the division of labour on Irish farms. We then turn to the work of women in the study areas and their understanding of their work roles. Based on their accounts and their relationship to the family farm, four categories of working relations are delineated, each associated with different kinds of constraints for the women concerned.

Divisions of Labour on Irish Family Farms

> To the woman falls the first duty of the day. She must rake together such live ashes as remain in the slaked turf fire in the hearth, put down new sods for the fire and rekindle the blaze. This done, she hangs the kettle on the hooks making ready for the first tea of the day. . . In the household the responsibility of day-to-day housekeeping belongs to the woman. Hers, too, is the care of the children. . . But her work stretches beyond the house door. In the morning after breakfast she takes the milk buckets and milks the cows in the sheds in the haggard. This is merely one of the many trips she makes in and out of the kitchen doors for fuel, or water, to feed and tend the animals and the fowl. Her milking finished, she must bring the milk in and separate it. . . The whole process of the conversion of milk to butter is her charge. . . All the care of the calves, pigs, and fowl falls to her lot. . . Her work ends only with the separating that takes place when she brings her milk into the house. Even then, while the men may sit round the fire talking over the day's work or the affairs of the community, she is not idle. . . When the whole family has finally gone off to bed, it is she who must close up the house at night and slake the fire in the hearth. (Arensberg and Kimball, 1968: 37–39)

Arensberg and Kimball's detailed ethnographic description of rural life in the west of Ireland in the 1930s is a unique record of the working life of farm women on the small peasant farms of the time. The situation they describe would have been little different on smallholdings in other parts of the country. Farming was very much a family operation in which all able-bodied members were involved. Women were responsible for the farmyard economy of milking, rearing of young animals (usually pigs and calves), poultry, butter making and frequently the cultivation of vegetables as well. On the small tillage plots typical of smaller holdings, they helped with crop cultivation (potatoes, turnips, beet) and often at haymaking and harvesting. All self-provisioning – butter making, fruit preservation as well as cooking and baking – was their responsibility. In addition they usually bore large families and had complete responsibility for childcare and household work. Women's work involved an endless round of chores virtually unchanging with the seasons and physically exhausting.

Family work was structured around gender and age, a 'concerted effort' within which there was a rigid division of labour between women and men (Arensberg and Kimball, 1968: 45). Animal husbandry, the buying and selling of animals, most fieldwork (e.g., ploughing, harrowing) and structural yard work (e.g., building, repairing) requiring heavy effort, was undertaken by the male 'farmer' whose work was much more varied and less restricted in space than that of the farm wife. The division of labour and power was sustained by beliefs and values based on what were considered the 'natural' attributes of each sex (1968: 48–49). Ridicule and derisiveness greeted those who breached sex-role boundaries, particularly when a man was seen to do a woman's work. Higher status and importance were attached to men's work, and they made all the major decisions related to the farm.

While Arensberg and Kimball have provided a valuable ethnographic description of familial arrangements on Irish family farms, their functionalist perspective (which portrayed the farm family as a harmonious haven of complementarity) led them to assume throughout that women themselves found this arrangement satisfactory and found 'reward and pleasure' in their work roles (1968: 46). We have no evidence of whether, or how, women contested their roles or the kind of sanctions which might be brought to bear by the wife in the event of her husband failing to fulfil his work obligations or provide adequately for the family. It would appear that she had few, being herself without property or an independent source of income, so that it was in her interest to ensure the smooth operation and maximum profitability of the farm and the goodwill of her husband. Nevertheless the very separateness of work roles and the independent control of a regular proportion of the farm income (the butter and egg money) as well as their control and influence over the children, may have at least conferred on women a kind of domestic autonomy. For instance Bourke (1991: 8) has suggested that wives' power in the household was considerable since they controlled the bulk of household expenditure which was spent on food. Refusal to cook a meal was also, she suggests, an important sanction used by women. A rigid division of labour may actually put limits on the exercise of patriarchal power, since women monopolise certain skills and knowledge (Connell, 1987: 125).

Whatever its limits, the Irish farm family as described by Arensberg and Kimball was strongly patriarchal with control of labour, property and succession in the hands of male farmers. The organisation of farm work was premised on a significant and constant input of the farm woman's labour. Her contribution to farm production was an essential part of her role as farm wife and was additional to her domestic and childcare responsibilities. Family farming as a social form therefore involved the incorporation of women's labour in farm production, and the well-being of the farm family was related to how effectively the farm wife executed her prescribed role. Her cooperation was assured by the fact that nothing less than her own and her children's present and future well-being depended on it. Reviewing Arensberg and Kimball's study, Hannan and Katsiaouni (1977: 20) observed that 'the whole pattern of family interaction, both as to the allocation of task roles and of power is such as to maintain the superordinate-subordinate relationship between spouses'. Indeed, Arensberg and Kimball's account of the internal structure of farm families is not unfamiliar to many contemporary farm wives, particularly those from smallholdings, who grew up in such circumstances and/or experienced them in the early days of their marriage. This was evident in Chapter Four from farm wives' comparisons with their mother's lives or their own early farming days, and will again be clear from the comments of the women recorded here.

The work of farm women on larger more prosperous farms in the east region in particular may not have been as arduous, mainly because of the presence of hired labour. Unfortunately, we do not have similar ethnographic evidence from these larger farms but we do know that hired farm and domestic labour was common (Breen, 1983; Fahey, 1990). Indeed one of the women from a relatively large farm in the present study suggested that her own life was much more difficult than that of her mother, observing that 'my mother and grandmother were women of leisure with a lot of help'. While the work of women may not have been so physically taxing as on smaller holdings, there is no reason to believe that the intra-family authority system of male dominance was any different, although it may have been exercised somewhat differently.

Farm Women and Farm Work

The conventional sociological distinctions between productive and reproductive work, and farm and domestic work are not easily recognised by farm women today. While they clearly see non-farm occupational waged work such as teaching or nursing as 'work', their concept of unpaid work is rather indistinct. Consequently, by taking on normative definitions of work, they underestimate the work they do, either by not defining it as work at all, or by blurring the distinction between work and leisure. Women in the west for instance said that working on the bog was physically hard but that they really enjoyed being out in the fresh air, having all the family involved and getting the fuel in for the winter (incorporating concepts of leisure, family and farm household reproduction in one work task). Since the range of work done on a family farm does not fit into the conventional wage-labour work model, it tends to get treated in much the same way as domestic work – as being part of a way of life rather than a job/work in the conventional sense. Women often 'talk down' the work that they do, comparing it to their mother's work which was much more difficult and physically taxing. In so far as they do make distinctions, the primary one is between 'inside' and 'outside' work. The latter can be either 'fieldwork' or 'yardwork', or work on the bog which is thought of as farm work. 'Inside work' includes both housework and childcare and household repairs and maintenance (such as decorating). Delphy and Leonard (1992: 202–3) have pointed out that French farm women make the same inside/outside work distinction.

Manual Work

Sixty percent of farm women in the west and 40 percent of those in the east were regularly involved in manual work on the farm. Dairying and market gardening are the most labour intensive enterprises and it is on farms with these enterprises that women are most heavily involved in manual work. On dairy farms their work is usually in the yard and centred on the milking (including preparing the cows and washing up afterwards), feeding the calves, as well as herding, and checking cattle:

> I do a bit of everything – feed calves, take over if he's not here milking and washing. I can take over completely if he is away. The kids go for the cows morning and evening, H milks and I do the washing up most days. It depends on what I have to do inside, some days I might not be able to get out. I feed the calves, I think women are better at this, more patient and more used to children. . . Men will take them or leave them, women are more fussy about them. I'd also be involved in moving and changing stock, weighing lambs, sorting out cattle for the headage. (Dairy farm, W30)

Women on dairy farms are strongly aware of the importance of their work partly because it is so visible but also because they know that they are virtually indispensable to the smooth running of the enterprise. The time and work commitment involved in twice-daily milking seven days a week for most of the year means that family labour is virtually essential. (The only farm wife on a dairy farm who was not involved in farm work in any way was a teacher with seven young children and her husband had other help on the farm). As one farm wife said: 'without my work he would have to work a lot slower and harder, he would have to be out earlier'. Yet most do not do the actual milking on a regular basis but are more involved in the preparation and washing up afterwards. Avoiding milking can be a deliberate strategy, as in the case of one respondent whose husband has an off-farm job. She explains it this way:

> I love working on the farm and do all the work except milking. I said early on that I would never milk because I would be tied to it forever more. The problem with dairy farming is that you are always tied to the farm. There is never a break – you always have to come home to milk. Dairying is a long hard slog, there must be easier ways of making money. I'm not from a dairy

farm and I thought [growing] potatoes was the hardest work until I got involved with cows. (Dairy farm, W15)

The predominant role of women on dairy farms is that of helper and the manual work that women do on these farms tends to be an extension of gender-specific household work – cleaning, tidying, feeding, organising. Care of young animals, mainly calves, is almost exclusively the woman's responsibility and women themselves see this as a gender-specific skill, attributing it to their greater patience and childcare experience:

When my mother-in-law got sick the men couldn't cope with the calves so H said that I would have to come down to the yard and I did. I like doing it. I am not from a farm but I had watched her doing it. Women are better with calves, they have a maternal instinct, know when a calf is ill or cold like they would with children. Men wouldn't even see it (Dairy farm, E24)

I feed the calves. They say that women are better than men at rearing calves but men don't like to admit this. (Dairy farm, E6)

Women are better at calf-rearing, especially dealing with sick calves. My husband wouldn't know. I'd make sure the calf would get its own milk, he wouldn't be as careful. There would be trouble if I didn't watch them and they might get scour or have to be put on medication. I wouldn't be blamed if the calf died but I'd be sorry. (Drystock farm, W7)

When farm families disengage from dairying, this is often precipitated by a wish to lessen the farm labour requirement, particularly when there is no other available family labour. Although this reduces the cleaning and tidying workload, women usually continue to look after the calves. On one farm where they had recently changed from dairying to drystock farming, the wife explained:

We got out of dairying in April 1990. It was too time consuming, we wanted to take it a bit easier as we are here on our own now. . . I bring in the cows in the morning for suckling and put the calves on them. I'd be tending to sick calves. . . That's all the work I do now, although I might give him a hand during the day with herding or if the vet was coming, or dosing. In the past I did much more. (Drystock farm, W5)

Certainly farm women are very conscious of the labour requirements of dairy farming and few would envisage themselves being able to run a dairy farm on their own:

I like farm work but I am doing less now than I used to. In the beginning there was no piped water and no machinery and H was away more. . . I often think that if anything happened to H, I wouldn't feel that I could continue on my own. I wouldn't be able to do the heavy work and if I had to pay someone, it wouldn't be feasible. I'd sell the stock and let the land. (Dairy farm, W12)

Market gardening too, makes huge labour demands on farm families, and in competitive market conditions family labour is a *sine qua non* of market gardening. The work is seasonal however, depending on the crop involved:

I pick and grade tomatoes from April to September. During July and August it would be from 6.30 am to 8.30 pm and at other times six to seven hours. H's brother takes the tomatoes to the market two or three times a day. I work five-and-a-half days per week. I insist on taking a half day Saturday. (Market gardening, E3)

Another older woman, who now considers herself retired as she is over sixty, said:

I am officially retired but I keep the books and I help out. I do all the grading [of vegetables] and select the staff in summer. I water plants, sow seed, all the easy jobs . . . I worked all the time picking tomatoes, planting, grading. We had flowers – tulips, daffodils, chrysanthemums . . . it was desperately hard work but we were young and we didn't mind it. We would be up at 6.00 am and often didn't finish until eleven at night. (Market gardening, E4)

In both dairying and market gardening the sheer urgency and physical demand of the manual work mean that the women involved are very conscious of their labour input. Because the family labour is so obviously crucial to the success of the enterprises, they have a sense of the teamwork involved in keeping the operation running smoothly and of the significance of their own contribution. Their involvement centres mainly around the yard and most have little direct input into what they call 'fieldwork' except to help out in emergencies. Driving the tractor seems to be the critical boundary between yard and field work, with most women saying they would not drive the tractor except in an emergency. Unwillingness to drive the tractor may have its roots in culturally prescribed gender roles but it also appears to be a way of resisting incorporation into a whole range of heavy work which women prefer to avoid. As one woman put it:

I don't drive the tractor, although I suppose I would if I had to. My husband has said to me that it's a pity you don't drive the tractor. Whatever has to be done you just do it and that's it. It depends on what makes money. (W13)

The gender division of work then seems to occur primarily between yard and fieldwork, with women confining their manual work primarily to the yard. This is borne out by the work roles of the women on farms in the east on which tillage was the main enterprise. These farms are highly commercialised with two being run in partnership arrangements with the husband's brother(s). The third was run by a couple who had experienced severe financial difficulties over the past several years. None of these women had a significant involvement in manual work but two of them had a significant non-manual involvement as we shall see below.

Drystock farming was by far the most common main enterprise in both east and west, accounting for two-thirds of all the farms studied. The labour requirements on drystock farms vary greatly depending on the size and intensity of the farm operation. The work involvement of women on such farms is related to the labour demands of the enterprise and also to the availability of other family labour, including that of their husbands. It can range from primary responsibility for managing the farm operation to almost complete detachment from it. Extensive involvement is generally associated with the husbands' engagement in off-farm work or having an illness which restricts their labour input:

> The system here is suckling cows and sheep. My husband got a heart attack seven weeks ago so I have been doing most of the farm work since then. My son helps with the heavy work in the evening. In the morning I milk a cow for the house and then let the calves to the cows, water and feed the cows. Then I count the stock and look at them. . . I check the stock during the day. Some of the sheep are three miles away and if he is not fit to drive I go over on the bicycle to check them. In the evening I do the same chores as morning. I always did my share before H got sick but he would manage on his own if I couldn't get out. (Drystock farm, W4)

> We have just cattle. I help with dosing, bring in the silage, check the stock to see if they are OK. Feeding them means going a mile and a half up the road as the farm is not here beside the house. (Drystock farm, E8, husband has off-farm job)

> I do everything and anything, I do the jobs as they come up and I have to do it. I feed calves, count cattle, sheep, help with lambing and so on. I like doing it, I would die in a town. . . The only job I don't do is drive the tractor. . . When the kids were small I didn't do as much because my father and mother-in-law were here. The farming was not as intensive then. I would say it is half and half between us as to the farm work. I put down housewife in the Census. I knew it was wrong, it's tradition I suppose. I don't know why. I suppose you feel you are downgrading your husband if you put down farmer. (Drystock farm, W6, husband has off-farm business)

Women were more involved in manual work on drystock farms in the west than in the east for a variety of reasons. Firstly, fewer wives were themselves involved in off-farm paid work and so were available to work on the farm. Secondly, almost twice as many husbands in the west were involved in off-farm work and all but three of these were on drystock farms. Incidentally, on the three dairy farms where husbands were working off the farm, their work was either part-time or structured in such a way that they were available on the farm for much of the day. Thirdly, drystock farms in the west are smaller, less intensive and more reliant on the labour input of the immediate family; there are no adult children (sons) working full time on these farms and hired help is rarely employed and even then, only on a casual basis on the bigger holdings. Perhaps more significantly, women's involvement in farm work in the west represents the last vestiges of the small-farm economy described at the beginning of this chapter. The farmyard economy of egg production and butter production has disappeared, but for many women this has happened only in the present generation:

> I had hens and loved them but they annoyed my husband around the dairy so we have not had them for fifteen years or so. I had ducks too, they were easy to rear and lovely to eat. . . I haven't made butter for years and I just used to make it for the house. As time went on we found that it didn't pay, you could buy butter cheaper. (W5)

> I made butter when I was younger and sold it to the local shop, but I gave it up. I don't remember why, it was too much trouble I suppose. (W3)

> We have no hens anymore . . . they are dirty and a nuisance and they wouldn't lay half the time. I don't like free-range eggs now that I have got used to the others. (W10)

The demise of the farmyard economy has not however pushed women on small holdings in the west back into the home but rather extended their involvement into other yard-based tasks with less rigid gender boundaries. They remain, however, in the private domain of farming, rarely engaging in public farm work such as attending livestock sales or open days, or representing the farm family at public meetings or in farming organisations. In fact very few of the women in either of the study areas were involved in organisations of any kind and those who were, tended to be those who were least involved in farm work.

The sense of engagement with the family farm (even on low-intensity drystock enterprises) which the accounts of women in the west convey, is in sharp contrast to several of those from the east, where the women are completely detached from the farm which they see as a business like any other. This is most common where wives come from non-farm backgrounds and/or have their own careers or businesses, but also on larger farms where labour is hired:

> I do none [farm work] at all. The only thing I do is stand at the road when they are loading cattle or give a hand at herding but that is only three times a year or so. I never did any [farm] work, nor did H's mother. (Large drystock farm, E5)

> I do no farm work and I never did any. I am the world's worst. I am interested in it I suppose in that it is part of our lives, but I don't like animals and the smells and the dirt. I associate it with old farmhouses and the smells in them. I don't do account-keeping or any other work, I suppose it is lack of interest really. (Drystock farm, E19, wife has own business)

> I don't do any, I just drive by. (Tillage, E21, wife has own business)

Non-Manual Work

Almost all farm women are involved in non-manual farm work in some way. This can range from the fairly typical tasks of dealing with callers, awaiting deliveries, running errands or discussing the farm business, to total financial management for the whole farm operation. Generally non-manual work casts women in a supportive rather than managerial role. It is 'inside work' in the same way as household work and childcare. Although it is farm work (in the sense that it would not be required if there were no farm) women often do not see it as such. The wife of a large tillage farmer in the east, herself from a non-farm background, described her involvement thus:

> I don't really do any farm work . . . apart from standing at gates or something like that when I might be needed. I drive in summer, bringing teas and dinners to the fields and doing errands. . . I deal with callers, say when people come for hay and straw, and any other callers to the house and answer the phone . . . if there is no one here for the phone it is bad. (Tillage, E1)

Being on call and available to help out when needed is typical of the non-manual role that many women play particularly on the larger farms and on farms where produce is being sold directly from the yard, as this requires that someone be available all the time. Even women who are in full-time paid work themselves sometimes take on this role:

> I make the phone calls and do all the errands and messages – the chemist, the vet and so on. I get the accounts ready for the IFAC [Irish Farm Accounts

Cooperative] recorder and pay most of the bills or they would be left here otherwise. (Tillage and sheep, E15, Teacher)

Usually though, when women are in full-time paid work, they tend to have a lesser involvement in all farm work, but they are available as a reserve and in emergencies. As is the case with manual work, it is the women who are at home all the time or whose husbands have off-farm work who tend to have the greatest involvement. One woman working on a dairy farm described her work involvement (both manual and non-manual) as follows:

> I do about twenty to thirty percent of the work, just the handy work! I sup-pose if you were to include all the paper work, I do about fifty percent in all. Every year there is more paperwork for cattle. H says you would need to take a suitcase to the mart with all the papers. (Dairy farm, W30)

A majority of wives in both areas are involved in account-keeping and financial management. On low intensity drystock farms and on the more intensive farms where an accountant or a professional farm account service is used, this may simply be a matter of keeping track of bills and receipts but it means that wives have an intimate and ongoing knowledge of the farm finances. In the following example, the respondent has a full-time job, nevertheless it is she who keeps the farm accounts. In recent years they have experienced financial difficulties in farming and this has made her acutely aware of the need for proper financial management:

> I keep farm records for the accountant. I'd know better than H and I have to know what is going on, what money is there for food, the kids' education and so on. At the moment we don't know what to do, the accountant and our adviser are going to sort it out. I'd like to go without counting pennies for once. (Drystock farm, E22)

Other wives take on a more proactive managerial role in relation to the farm finances, usually explaining their involvement in terms of men's incompetence or unwillingness to take on the tedious work involved. This level of involvement is associated with commercialised farms where tight financial management is essential:

> I do all the books and when a problem arises I figure it out. Men haven't a clue [her husband and son]. When the accountant or IFAC ring up H puts them on to me. If I died in the morning I tell them they would end up in Mountjoy [prison], they are both the same. H only saw the accountant once when he had to. . . H was ill nine years ago and I had to do it then, so he left

it to me. Women are better at balancing the books, they see further ahead. When there is any investment needed I'd be asked. (Dairy farm, E18)

I don't do anything outside but do all the farm accounts and financial management for the farm, see the adviser, run errands etc. If they want a new tractor they come to me and Mum is supposed to find the money. . . There was a bank strike and when it was over everything was in a mess so I just took over. My husband just didn't want to bother. I'm better at it and I have more education. A lot of women are keeping accounts, they are always there in the house and men want to be outside. I am the banker for the house and farm but it has its disadvantages, like the times when they want to buy things and I have to say no. I could always threaten to throw it there and say, 'see for yourselves', but it would never come to that because they really don't want to have to do all that paperwork. . . The men don't like keeping books, even the lads who have the Green Cert.[3] will leave it to me. (Large drystock farm, W3)

I do all the talking to the bank manager, H lacks confidence. He comes with me but he doesn't open his mouth. . . I write all the cheques here and have learned to forge my husband's signature. I pay all the bills. It is an escape for him, he calls me his financial advisor but it means I have to face the music and I get all the hassle. (Market gardening, E13)

While these women clearly recognise their own competence in financial management, they also see that it is in their husbands' interest to hand over the tedium and stress involved in such work to someone else whom they can trust. Indeed the last woman quoted above was actually negotiating the sale of a part of the farm at the time of the interview, as the farm business was under severe financial pressure. It also allows the men to opt out of ongoing financial management but clearly demands a conjugal contract based on high levels of mutual trust and reciprocity. Although these wives, in having taken over the farm finances in this way, are acting in a managerial rather than secretarial role, they are a minority. Most women who are involved in account-keeping explain their involvement more in terms of it being a shared task, and see their own role as that of helper rather than manager. Those least likely to be involved in account-keeping are those who have their own off-farm jobs or businesses.

It is clear then that farm women are involved in a wide variety of farm work. Their degree of involvement is influenced by a complex of factors which are structured, inter alia, by the particular circumstances of the family farm, the nature of the marital relationship and their own preferences. In general, women have a greater involvement in manual work on farms with more labour intensive systems such as dairying and market

3. Certificate of vocational qualification in farming in Ireland.

gardening where the success of the enterprise is essentially premised on the availability of family labour. But even on these farms, their involvement is in turn influenced by whether they are working off the farm; the availability of other labour; the patterns of involvement established from early in their marriage; and their own preferences. Women's work is carried out mainly in the farmyard and farmhouse rather than the fields, so that they are least likely to be involved in manual work on tillage farms. In general, women in the west conveyed a greater sense of engagement with farm work and farming as a livelihood. This reflects not only the differences in the nature of the farm economies between the two regions but also differences in the farm cultures, women's backgrounds, and off-farm work commitments of both spouses.

Having established the range of work performed by women on family farms, we now turn to the context in which such work is carried out. It is not so much the nature of the work which is important in understanding how farm women are subordinated, but rather the work relationship and how it is constituted. Do men/farmers control the work that women do? What rewards do women receive for their work? Do women always carry out such work in a subordinate relationship to their husbands or does negotiation involve a redistribution of power?

Rewards for Farm Work

Whatmore has argued that three of the most important dimensions of the patriarchal labour relations in the family farm are farm women's limited legal and financial interest in the family farm, their restricted involvement in farm decision-making and lack of control over the money generated from the farm business (1991: 82). Women on farms may do as much (or more) farm work as their husbands, or indeed be responsible for managing the farm as a business, and yet have no ownership rights to the family farm, no significant say in farm decision-making and no control over the farm income. This too is the core of Delphy and Leonard's contention regarding women's work in the family, that is that the essence of women's exploitation lies in the fact that they do not own what they produce within the family; the products of their labour belong to the head of household, i.e., in farm households, the farmer (1992: 89).

The patrilineal system of inheritance ensures that, with few exceptions, the only women who own land in their own right are widows and this is borne out in the present study. While a majority of farms in both east and west were owned solely by husbands, there are quite striking differences between the two areas in that the proportion in joint ownership was almost three times higher in the west. In the west 63 percent (19/30) of farms were registered in the husband's name only; 27 percent (8/30) were in joint names and, of the remaining three farms, two were owned by widows and the third had been transferred to a son. In the east, 83 percent (25/30) of the farms were owned solely by husbands and only 10 percent (3/30) were owned jointly, and the remaining two farms were owned by widows.

Involvement in decision-making reflects a somewhat similar pattern. On farms in the east, farm decisions were made by the couple jointly on 27 percent (8/30) of the farms, compared to 43 percent (13/30) in the west. A much higher proportion of couples in the west had joint bank accounts – two-thirds as opposed to one-third in the east. Thus, although the predominant situation is one of subordination, there are, especially in the west, a significant proportion of farms where wives have proprietary rights, are involved in joint decision-making, and have access to the couple's joint income. This is consistent with the earlier observation of a higher level of farm work involvement among women in the west.

While these regional differences are striking, differential rewards appear also to be influenced by the size of the farm operation, the system of farming, and wives' other work commitments. What is clear is that some women have evolved a conjugal arrangement with their husbands whereby, in relation to the operation of the farm at least, they have managed to negotiate a considerable lessening of their subordination. This situation is quite different from Delphy and Leonard's interpretation of the situation of wives on French family farms (1992: 205–7). There is considerably more variation than the straightforward patriarchal regime, characterised by complete male dominance and control over all farm decisions and money, that they describe.

What women say about farm work best captures this. Those who have negotiated a joint or sharing arrangement see themselves as being involved in a partnership, and use the terms 'we' and 'ours' to refer to the farm as opposed to 'his' or 'theirs':

> Money is thrown up on the shelf and we help ourselves until it is gone. While it is there the two of us use it. . . I don't think of it as payment. I say I'm an unpaid servant. . . Of course I'd like regular payment, who wouldn't, but not from the farm. It's not like that on a farm. (W6)

> I love working on the farm. . . The farm work is the least I could do because he is out working for most of the day. All the money we make here is shared and I consider it pay for the work I do. My husband appreciates it and sometimes tells me so. (W15)

We work well together. The lads [her husband and brother-in-law] are inclined to say 'we'll do this' and I'll say, 'let's think it through and look at all the options' . . . the three of us will talk it out and it will be a better decision. I think they do appreciate me, they will consult me on everything. (E3)

I see us as partners, it is all joint. . . We discuss farm decisions – like when H was buying a tractor, I said, do you need all the tractors, so we traded in two against a new one. The same with buying cattle, we discuss it. (E7)

These comments contrast with those of the farm wives who clearly perceive themselves to be in a subordinate role:

I don't mind farm work although sometimes I get sick of it. I like getting away from housework but dairying is an awful tie. No matter what time you get to bed you have to get up in the morning. . . We really don't think of the money we get from the farm as payment for work. It really is different from a job where you have a wage coming in every week. I put down housewife in the Census, I don't know why really, I suppose I don't realise what I do. . . The farmer's wife's work is not recognised, people don't realise what we do, the long hours, the hard work. Our work is taken for granted by everyone including husbands. Men have long hours too, all around the clock. It is a long day and there are ups and downs. (W18)

I am not the farm manager, I would always ask him. I would consult him first but I am involved in decisions and would call the vet and deal with him and other callers. . . I would love to have been a farmer if I was a boy but my brother is at home now. In those days it was one of the boys who got the farm. (E11)

Other women perceive their subordinate role as being reinforced by ideological and institutional factors outside of the micro level of the farm family, whereby their work is not recognised and they are not considered as work units in the tax or social security system:

We each have an account. Most of the money goes into H's account and I have a small account for myself. . . I don't see the money in my account as payment, I regard the farm as a business. . . I think there should be a tax allowance for the farmer's wife as they share the work also. I feel I'm doing as much for the farm as the others. (W3)

I don't like farm work, I do it because it is there . . . like having to milk. You are really tied with cows. . . I think the housewife should be entitled to some income, not dole. There are so many men on the dole, no one mentions the women. Their work is not recognised. People ask me if I am working and I say no. (W10)

I am completely unpaid [for the work on the farm]. I sometimes complain to them but when I look at the hours they work. . . H is out in the yard at 6.30 am every morning and sometimes doesn't come in until nine at night . . . People don't understand how hard you work in farming. . . I think there should be something for the wife, there is no allowance for the wife's work in the tax system, they are not one unit of labour. It has nothing to do with money, it's about being recognised – I handle the money anyway. . . Ours is family money, they take what I give them. (E18)

All women are classed as equal nowadays, although I always felt I was equal to any man. I considered my father and my husband as the boss but I expected them to discuss things with me . . . I put down housewife in the census, I don't know why. What else could I put down? Down the years it was the husband who was the farmer if the land was in his name. (E23)

The rewards for farm work are not then the same for all farm women. There is considerable variation in women's relationship to the family enterprise, the nature of the conjugal contract and their own understanding of that relationship. We return to these issues later in this chapter but first we turn to household work and its place in the lives of farm women.

Household Work

All of the women in the study had responsibility for household work and all but one were mothers and had primary responsibility for childcare. When childcare and household work are combined with regular involvement in farm work it often means that women work all of their waking hours, moving between all three spheres through the course of the day, as in the following examples:

8.00 to 8.30 am get up and get children ready for school and prepare breakfast. Then go out to the yard and feed calves, wash up and clean up after the milking. Return inside and wash dishes and tidy the house. Then H returns [he has risen earlier, milked and then worked in paid job for two hours] and we have a cup of tea. Then we both go out and work around the farm. Sometime after half eleven I come in to get the dinner and eat around half one to two o'clock. Then I tidy up, do the washing and ironing before going to the school to pick up the two younger children and bring my mother-in-law milk. Then it is home to give the kids their dinner, wash up and then get the eldest girl from secondary school at four. When she has had her dinner I go out again to wash the milk tank and buckets for the evening milking, collect the cows and feed the calves. After the milking I get the tea for H and myself, the kids help themselves. At around eight I would be checking the homework and then prepare the clothes and shoes and get the washing organised for the next day. By then it is time for bed,

I watch very little TV. (Dairy farm, husband has part-time job, three children, W15)

During the pregnancies I worked until the day I went to the hospital and then I brought the babies with me with a bottle in my pocket. I had a wooden box that I put them all into and a pram. Then later they played around the yard while we worked. All the neighbouring kids used to come here because we had a safe yard. I used to do my housework from eight to nine in the morning. (Market gardening, five children, E4)

Even when women are not as involved in farm work as those quoted above, they have to cope with a whole set of conditions associated with the occupation of farming. These range from the stresses associated with uncertain or inadequate incomes and the vagaries of the weather, to the irregularity of the working hours of their husbands, their distance from facilities and services, and the constant demands of crops and animals. Housework for most farm women does not just involve cooking, laundry, cleaning, shopping and childcare but often includes other tasks such as painting and decorating, gardening, mending, baking (especially bread), and jam-making.

In common with women elsewhere (Oakley, 1974; Edgell, 1980; Whatmore, 1991), most of the women studied dislike housework – finding it tedious, relentless and unrewarding. No other topic yielded such uniformity of responses. Those who said that they liked housework explained that what they liked was the end result – a clean and tidy house – rather than the actual tasks which had to be carried out to achieve it, although a small minority said that they enjoyed the actual work. Most of the women said that they liked cooking, which at least afforded them some creativity and the satisfaction of seeing their families enjoy what they had prepared. While being unequivocal about how much they disliked housework, they did appreciate the autonomy and control over tasks (however monotonous) which it allowed:

It has to be done, I just do it. I hate making the beds. There is nothing good about it. You clean things and then they get dirty again. . . I have to hoover everyday. Cooking is not great, I'm just an average cook, I don't mind it. (E1)

I hate it. What do you achieve with it? It has to be done. I keep it clean and that is it. The repetition is the worst and the loneliness in one sense. There is no interaction, it is a solitary thing. There is nothing good about it that I know of. (E5)

It is a necessary evil, like clockwork I just do it. The worst is coming in from outside and making dinner and cleaning up . . . it takes such a long time. The best bit is that I don't have to do what I did yesterday . . . having control, I can decide what to do. (E7)

What I think of housework is unprintable. Housework to me is dull, dreary and repetitive and thankless and needs no brainwork. The worst is having to do it. I hate housework. I don't mind painting and decorating but I hate washing up and so I bought a dishwasher. There is nothing good about it with three small kids, you tidy and then they untidy, there is no come back you just do it over again. I like when the job is finished and the place is neat and tidy. (E23)

I like things to be well organised and well run and do the housework to achieve that end, I don't like actually doing it . . . but I hate an untidy house. (W1)

I think it is time consuming and a total waste of energy and time and I do as little as possible. (W22)

The primary responsibility for housework and childcare remains with farm women. Although there are exceptions, farm men in general have very little involvement in household work, except as the women put it, 'when I'm not there'. Women however do not necessarily see this as a natural state of affairs, constantly pointing to the way in which younger, particularly non-farm, couples share domestic work. Older women rationalise men's non-involvement in terms of culture and tradition and the role patterns established by his own family of origin. Younger women usually explain their husbands' lack of involvement by referring to farm work commitments not allowing time for housework, men's inefficiency at household tasks, and the fact that by not ever having lived away from home they have never 'learned' to do housework:

H wouldn't mind doing housework but he has enough to do outside. (E10)

H will dry the dishes and change the baby but I prefer to do it myself. I can't stand to see him half doing it. . . My husband was never in a flat, he never had to cook or clean. Guys that have been out in flats are better and H was never a nine to five person. (E14)

Nowadays when the two people in a couple are out working they share the housework. On a farm you don't expect it. (W4)

H can cook if I am away but leaves such a mess that I would hurry home to do it myself. I suppose women do the housework because they are the ones inside. H is gone most of the day. (W15)

Most women describe their husbands as undertaking housework or childcare only when they are not available themselves. They recognise the strategies which men have adopted to avoid housework, such as not seeing what needs to be done, or doing the work less efficiently in order to avoid displaying any competence:

> I don't think men will do fifty percent of the housework or childcare in any circumstances. Anyone who thinks they will is only dreaming. Women do the housework – that's the way in Irish society, it is conditioning. You really can't change people, I flare up over the dishes, he will say he is doing them and it drives me mad to see him doing them slowly and wrong, leaving things and putting them away where I can't find them. I do it myself and I'll be quicker. He says: 'leave that and I'll do it later', and it drives me mad as I want them done now so I give him the baby to mind and do them myself. . . It is how he was brought up, he couldn't boil a kettle. . . If men are living in flats or had to do it at home it is different – like my own brothers who are much better. (E7)

> H helps with the housework, he would feed the kids and clean up if I were gone. He often got down and scrubbed the floor, and he'd always have himself and the kids fed when I'd come in from town. He wouldn't be waiting for me to come home and do it. He often would help, but to be honest I'd have it done myself while he'd be messing at it! (W9)

Women of course adopt their own strategies to involve men in 'women's work' as in the following instance:

> H never changed a nappy but he was good for feeding and would sit for hours with a small baby. When the babies were small I used to get up early on a Sunday morning and steal out so as not to wake the baby. When I'd be going out the front door I'd bang it so that the baby would wake up and he would have to feed it. It would be fed when you come home so it would be one less job. I never told that to H until lately and he never realised what I was doing. (W6)

The men who help most are those who come from atypical households where their mothers did not perform the traditional female roles:

> H is good at housework, just as good as me. He lost his mother at eleven and is fantastic in the kitchen. When I was sick and in hospital for nine weeks during the pregnancy, he was fantastic, the house was perfect when I got home. He changed all the children and fed them. He washed and ironed my nightdresses when I was in hospital. He is very good with the kids, with their schoolwork etc., even more patient than I am. (W16)

> H can cook and do anything. His mother was sick when he was a child and was away a lot so he had to fend for himself. How much he does depends on who is nearest the stove . . . especially when he is at home. (W27)

These latter two men are exceptions, but not just in an Irish context. Research in other countries has shown that there has been no substantial increase in men's involvement in domestic work in a variety of circumstances (see Morris, 1990: 80–102 for an extensive review). Most farm women have an air of resignation about men's involvement in household work but not in childcare. Younger women insist that men do have a greater involvement in parenting, reflecting the shifts in ideologies and values about the role of the father which were referred to in the previous chapter. The amount of housework which women do, their feelings about it and the standards of housework which they believe are desirable appear to be related to the amount of time available for it and their own personal preferences.

While women do most of the domestic tasks, the majority are either involved in farm work or in off-farm work in addition to their domestic responsibilities, thus carrying the typical double burden. Only 17 percent (5/30) of women in the west and 13 percent (4/30) in the east are housewives in the conventional meaning of the term. Oakley's distinction between feelings about housework and orientation to the housewife role is relevant here (1974: 184–87). The minority of women in each area who are engaged in full time housework are also the most positively oriented to the housewife role. However, it is not the role of housewife which provides their primary identity, but that of mother – an issue which is dealt with in a later chapter.

The Working Relationship – Four Categories

Four distinct types of working relationship emerge from the way in which the women themselves talk about their involvement in family farming. Such a typology can be seen as a way of incorporating several critical aspects of the gendered work organisation of family farming including the actual work performed by women; their understanding of that work; the way in which their work roles subordinate them; and how this is related to the conjugal contract between the spouses. As in all distinctions of this kind, these four role types are of necessity slightly reified and the lines between them are not so clear in reality.

Working for the Family Farm

The work roles of thirteen women in the west and eleven in the east can be understood as 'working for the family farm'. This means being involved in a partnership (usually but not exclusively with their husbands) in a range of tasks and decisions and perceiving the farm as a family enterprise. In this situation women's sense of involvement in the farm as a business and in farming as an occupation is very strong. All but three (all in the east) came from farming backgrounds but their circumstances vary considerably. Factors associated with their major input to the farm include the fact that their husbands 'married in' to their (wives') family farms; their husbands have off-farm jobs; they are widowed; but, most typically in this category, husband and wife work jointly on the farm in sharing tasks and responsibilities. These working partnerships are more common in, but not exclusive to, the more labour-intensive systems such as dairying or market gardening where wives are involved in farm work on a day-to-day basis.

These women are fully involved in all aspects of the farm operation in terms of management and decision-making, although there may be certain tasks that they do not undertake. They talk of farm work in terms of something that they enjoy and to which they bring certain skills. They identify strongly with the farm as a business operation and/or a way of life. They speak of the satisfaction of seeing animals thriving, of sharing tasks, and of being involved in a family project. They have a strong appreciation of the lifestyle of farming, of 'being your own boss'. When describing difficult times or discussing falling prices in agriculture they do so in terms of 'we', and of how the family might respond or be affected. Those who have been through serious financial crises describe a joint approach to negotiations with banks and financial institutions, while in some cases the women themselves take on the role of financial controller:

> He doesn't handle any money at all. I get all the money and manage how it is spent. We have a joint bank account since we got married and everything else is in joint names. It's a what's mine is yours and what's yours is mine situation. (W4)

> I deal with everything and the accountant was sending letters here addressed to H. I take that as an insult and I told him one day to put both names on the letters. I am the financial controller, I deal with bills, write cheques and see the bank manager and deal with the accountant. (E18)

Generally the women in this category look after the book-keeping and farm accounts, again attributing this to the special skills of women – better at budgeting, balancing the books, planning ahead. They see farm income as a family, rather than individual, reward for effort. Farm income is usually irregular and inadequate so that the preoccupation is more often with actual income generation rather than allocation.

As in all categories, women here have primary responsibility for domestic work and childcare but they see farm work as a way of 'escaping' from housework which is uniformly regarded as tedious and boring. Most say they would rather be 'out' than inside:

> I love being outside to tell you the truth. . . Working with animals you see some success from your work and you have your own time, you're not tied to the clock. . . I think of the income from the farm as payment for the work that both of us do here. (W30)

They say that one of the advantages of farming is that you can take the children with you when you work, and among older women, mothers-in-law played a significant role in childminding and domestic help. Childcare responsibilities do affect the degree to which women can become involved in farm work, but for women in this category such responsibilities are not seen as an insurmountable obstacle to involvement in farm tasks. Their involvement in farm work only lessens when they take on part-time work off the farm, when they get older or when there is a change to a less intensive enterprise.

Women who work for the family farm do not perceive themselves to be subordinated by this in any way, but have created out of their involvement in farming a strong sense of identity with the family enterprise. They have a firm belief in the significance of their contribution to the family farm and a sense of solidarity with their husbands and other family members, who they perceive as having to work as hard as themselves for no more personal gain. Although they experience the 'triple burden' of childcare, domestic work and farm work, they do not feel victimised by it. Rather they contrast the ease with which they can move between areas of work to the segmented lives of women in paid employment. While they recognise that the work of farm women remains hidden and largely unnoticed, they understand this in terms of a set of macro-patriarchal structures through which all women are subordinated. In their own sphere, this seems irrelevant. These women are quite unconcerned, for instance, as to whether they are registered owners of the family farm, although many in fact are. Similarly, while they realise that men's virtual non-involvement in housework is neither desirable nor attributable to any 'natural' division of labour, they are realistic about the weight of culture and tradition and the role patterns established in the men's own family of origin. At any rate, the women convey no sense of regarding the reproductive work in which they are involved as being of less value than farm work.

The Farm Helper

> H has the cheque book and always had control of it. I never really questioned it or asked to have my name on the cheques, I suppose I felt the farm was his and it was his money . . . even though in my house it was my mother who controlled the money. Isn't it funny that I did it a different way. (E25)

> Whatever has to be done you just do it and that's it. . . When H was sick I realised I didn't even know how to put diesel in the car. . . I'd hate to think I would laze around here and not take responsibility. I made clothes and knit for the children and all that helps. Whenever I do spend money on myself, which is not often, like buying something or going to visit my mother, I'd say to myself aren't I entitled to it. (W13)

Women whom I have categorised as 'farm helpers' (seven in the west and six in the east) may contribute the same amount of labour to the farm as those working for the family farm but have less involvement in decision-making and less access to farm income. While they enjoy the lifestyle of farming, they may resent the work involved as well as the lack of independence and the sense of having no choice. They are on call all the time but speak of the farm as being 'his' and 'theirs' rather than 'ours'. They are attached to it by virtue of their labour but have never incorporated it as their own. Husbands control the farm income and are the sole owners of the farm. Although the farm woman may be contributing up to half of the farm work it is in the subordinate role of helper. This is closely related to the nature of the conjugal contract and an established pattern of control on the part of the husband who never has any involvement in housework and minimal involvement in child-care. Such women will often describe their husbands (and themselves) as old-fashioned:

> We have no discussions about the farm. H makes all the decisions and looks after the money and the banking of it. The house and the farm are in his name. Does it bother me? Yes. Farm women are getting a raw deal although I know not everyone is the same. You want your own independence and women have more of that now and it's no harm for women. (W24)

These women have a strong consciousness of being constrained by patri-archal power relations and of having established a pattern of inferiority throughout their married lives which is almost impossible to change. Their feelings about this are expressed as lack of independence, not having their own money, not having a say in decisions, being taken for granted and so on. Not all are equally explicit about this, nor do all appear to have a strongly contested conjugal relationship.

The Farm Homemaker

> I was never interested in farm work and never did any. . . I did bits and pieces growing up but I was the oldest so I was always working inside. (W11)

> I love housework. I like doing things here and I have the car, I can go where I like, I'm not tied to the house. I like all housework. The only thing I hate is cleaning windows. I like getting it all done before the kids get home and having the evening free. (E26)

There are five farm women in the west and four in the east whom I have categorised as 'farm homemakers'. Although they are available when needed, these farm women have very little ongoing involvement with work on the farm and are primarily home centred. Being on a farm may be regarded by them as almost incidental, particularly where the husband has (or had) off-farm employment. In such families the main source of income and identity is the non-farm occupation rather than farming, and such women do not think of themselves primarily as farmers' wives. In both west and east the other predominant characteristic of this category is that the farm woman does not see any need to get involved in the farm either because there is already enough labour, or she has never been encouraged to do so by her husband:

> I do none [farm work] at all. . . To tell the truth I've enough to do in the house and anyway my husband never expected me to work outside. He has enough help and I'd be seen as interfering. (E5)

Although not all these women profess to like housework, childcare and domestic work are the main focus of their working lives. They are house-centred rather than farm-centred, the house being the focal point of their work activities. They receive a 'housekeeping' allowance from their husbands and usually have very little money of their own. They talk of having to ask for money, and of really missing having their own money even though they may have a joint bank account with their husbands.[4]

Many of these women are involved in informal services outside the household such as taking care of old people, or assisting people who have no means of transport. They are more likely than other categories to be involved in organisations such as the ICA which they see as a way of getting out of the house and relieving the boredom and monotony of housework. It is also a way of creating a personal involvement away from

---

4. This issue of distribution of resources within the farm family will be dealt with in the next chapter.

home. The key differentiating feature of this category is their relative detachment from the farm although they are always available as reserve labour and to do errands associated with the farm. In this respect they are no different from the wives of other self-employed workers.

Farm Women in Paid Work

Five[5] farm women in the west and nine in the east were involved in full-time paid work. Three of those in the west were teachers, one managed the family pub and the fifth was an accounts clerk. All of these women had been raised on farms. In the east there were two teachers, three nurses, one laboratory technician and three who operated their own businesses. Four of these had no farming background. Apart from two women who had developed small businesses after marriage, and one who had taken over the family pub, all had retained their pre-marriage occupations throughout, rather than disengaging from and then later returning to paid work. They are a distinct and privileged category, not only in terms of the 'cultural capital' that they bring to the marriage but because their involvement in a distinct occupation outside the farm changes not only the character of the family labour process but also the nature of the conjugal relationship. By generating an income of their own, these women are in a much stronger position to challenge male domination in their relationships.

Working off the farm also changes their relationship to the family enterprise. For it is their occupational work, rather than the farm enterprise, which is central to their lives, both for the income it yields, and the strongly felt occupational identity and sense of self-worth associated with it. Generation of a personal income is a critical means of ensuring that they have secured what they consider to be a desirable standard of living. Indeed their marriage to a farmer is often premised on the expectation that it is their own earning power which will provide them with the material means to satisfy their aspirations:

> You have to have a certain standard in the house. . . It is not realistic to expect a living from a farm like this, and you just won't make money. I enjoy my job and we have a good quality of life, it is a good balance. (W22)

This was particularly the case in the west where off-farm income is often crucial on small holdings. Such women's contribution to the farm family income allows them a personal independence and higher material stan-

5. One woman in the west and two in the east who were involved in casual part-time work off the farm are not included here.

dard of living than their neighbours and protects the family from the risks associated with the uncertainty and unpredictability of farm income:

> It's very important to me to have my own money. I wouldn't like to be dependent at all. I spend the money on the housekeeping, the kids and myself and H pays the bills like ESB [electricity] and the phone. I would hate to be asking for money, it's very demoralising although some couples have a great understanding about this and just draw on what money they have. My own money is very important, our standard of living would be much lower if we didn't have it. It's a steady income, there every week, not like in farming. (W14)

> My income is nearly all that's available, even though it would probably be less than half of the income coming in. But we have a lot of commitments here. . . I couldn't live like that [if I had to ask for money]. If I see something I want I have the cheque book. In other jobs the income is coming in every week so the husband will probably give a certain amount [to the wife], but in farming you could go for weeks and have nothing. The cheque for the cattle mightn't be as much as he thought and then what happens . . . in other jobs it is easier to budget. (W29)

In each of these farms, the wife was a very significant contributor to the total family income – in some cases in excess of fifty percent. The importance of their contribution to the family income strengthens their negotiating position in the conjugal relationship with regard to their husband's participation in housework and childcare:

> H is willing to do housework and it is easy to do as much as me. When I am working he does more. It has to be like that, he takes over. I'm the main income earner here, I wouldn't be able to do it unless he was supportive. (W22)

None of these women had any significant involvement in the actual physical work on the farm and in some cases were quite detached from it, seeing it as an occupation like any other, or as a nuisance – 'all work and no profit' (in one case). Whereas on smaller holdings in the west, women's income was often crucial in ensuring farm continuity, in the larger more commercial holdings in the east, the income was less materially important, except in cases where the farm was under financial pressure. In such cases women's capacity to generate an independent income takes on a new significance and women themselves experienced this as additional responsibility:

> My job accounts for most of the money coming into the house now, about seventy percent. I couldn't stay at home. I have to go out and work. . . I feel pressure to work but I don't know if I could give up the wage packet either. (E22)

Even where there is critical financial pressure, women's incomes go to 'run the house' and/or pay the mortgage so that they have much more significant control over consumption than in cases where there is direct competition for the farm income between farm and home. Each has her own bank account and a strong awareness of the financial autonomy and security associated with this:

> I would miss having my own money, I wouldn't like to give up my job. Not having your own money makes you completely dependent, and what if anything happens to your husband. (E15)

These women are also career oriented and speak of the fulfilment and satisfaction that they get from their occupations as well as the benefits of getting out of the house and interaction with work colleagues. They also appreciate the benefits of farming as a lifestyle and as a desirable environment for raising children.

The Significance of the Four Categories

In examining the working relationship in family farms, four distinct categories of women emerge which are structured on the basis of their involvement in family farming as an enterprise and their own understanding of that involvement. Those classified as 'working for the farm' appear to have developed a particular way of contesting patriarchal structures by creating their own sphere of influence within the farm family. This is centred on their commitment to the family enterprise and is negotiated through a particular kind of conjugal or family contract, characterised by joint control and influence over the assets of the family enterprise. While the work regime is not necessarily characterised by egalitarian sharing of all tasks, the work relationship is such as to suggest a substantial lessening of the constraints associated with patriarchal power. On these farms there has been a significant erosion of male authority so that the women have a considerable influence, not just on day-to-day production and consumption, but on the future of the family farm. This is signified by their involvement in decision-making and financial management. Such arrangements in everyday working life make divisions between productive and reproductive work, and paid and unpaid work, meaningless to these women, and of questionable value theoretically for understanding their situation. Commitment to the family enterprise does not extend, however, to 'surviving at all costs'. Those on smallholdings are pragmatic about the future for family farming, and accept that the next generation will engage in farming only on a part-time basis. Even on the larger commercial holdings, where there will be a continuance of commercial farming into the next generation, most do not envisage a replication of the present family labour process, expecting that at least one half of the conjugal couple will be pluriactive. None see their daughters as performing the same vocational role, except in the context of choosing farming as an occupation with a desirable lifestyle.

Those who are 'farm helpers' feel much more constrained. They regard the farm enterprise as their husband's domain, in which they have (sometimes unwillingly) become involved. They perceive themselves as the anachronistic remains of an authoritarian system in which they are assigned to the role of helper in the farm and wife and mother in the home, a role model increasingly unacceptable to younger generations. As we shall see in a later chapter, they are actively shaping an alternative future for their children.

Farm homemakers are quite detached from the farm as a family enterprise and are almost completely confined to the domestic sphere. In this sense they are little different from the wives of other self-employed workers. They are not, however, detached from family farming as a social form since their regulation of domestic work and reproductive role are critical to farm continuity.

Farm women in paid work may provide the farm family with a regular source of income which can be essential for the survival of the family enterprise. Such women use their financial independence to obtain, in the first instance, a higher material standard of living for the family and to retain considerable control over consumption. They also use this independence to negotiate a more egalitarian distribution of work roles, reflecting more 'modern' ideologies of marriage, but not always successfully. On larger commercial farms women's incomes are less significant to the maintenance of the family farming enterprise. Such women use their occupational status to detach themselves from the farming enterprise, relating to it as an occupational category rather than to a family business of which they perceive themselves to be part. However, unlike the farm homemaker, these women's detachment and personal autonomy is underpinned by their own earning power.

By objective criteria and from a feminist perspective, family farming can be seen as oppressive to women. Their work is ignored in official statistics, apparently unpaid, and hidden in a social form in which farming and male(ness) are synonymous. In this chapter, the way in which the patriarchal structure extends to the private sphere of the family farm has been investigated. While there is ample evidence of patriarchal gender relations in the organisation of work and capital which are at their most extreme among those I have categorised as 'farm helpers', there is also much evidence of the ways in which women have managed to lessen the constraints of patriarchy through becoming active partners in the farm business or through working off the farm. We have already been able to discern some of the implications for consumption within the family. In the next chapter then we shift the focus to the farm family and the distribution of resources within it.

6

INSIDE THE FARM FAMILY

Distribution of resources

Introduction

In the previous chapter the focus on women's work involved looking inside the family farm, and at production which occurs both on the farm and in the household. This revealed considerable diversity in working arrangements, in the ways in which women are constrained, and in the ways they contest patriarchal structures and create their own spheres of influence. In this chapter we shift the focus to the farm family and to consumption, since the ultimate purpose of all labour, paid or unpaid, both on and off the family farm, is to provide the family with its desired consumption needs. We are concerned with consumption in the sense of ownership of, access to, and use of family resources, and specifically with the distribution of resources inside the family and how this is structured by gender. But also, as in the case of production, consumption structures gender, in that women are associated with consumption in a different way from men. They mainly perform the primary consumption-related tasks of budgeting, shopping, cooking, and caring. At the same time, access to household resources (such as money or food) may be structured asymmetrically on the basis of gender (Charles and Kerr, 1987). To allow for the possibility of family members enjoying different levels of consumption is of course a direct challenge to the idea of the household as a 'unit of consumption'. While it may be evident that household members consume unequally, mainstream studies of consumption have not even hinted at such differences and their relationship to gender issues (Delphy and Leonard, 1992).

Clearly this is an area of great complexity where day-to-day allocations between family members occur within the context of a familial ideology and are based on taken-for-granted assumptions, negotiations, and conflicts in which household members have unequal bargaining powers. Family households are, after all, arenas of both cooperation and conflict (Wilson, 1991). Moreover, in farm family households at least some (and perhaps all adult) family members are producing, earning and consuming in one location. On the one hand, the family may be suffused with ideologies of sharing, whereby farm income may be looked on as 'family' money rather than the earnings of 'the farmer', as we have seen in Chapter Five. Accumulation strategies, on the other hand, may favour the farm over the family. Ideologies of the male as farmer and patrilineal inheritance may mean that the accumulation of land and capital effectively channels family assets away from women.

It is important then to comprehend how gender as a social division within farm families structures farm women's access to family resources. In order to do this, we turn to ownership of land and property and access to money and other material resources. The terms on which each member of the farm couple enter farming are, of course, quite different and unequal – women usually enter farming by marrying a man who has acquired (or will eventually acquire) the family patrimony by gift or inheritance. This creates the basis for an uneven distribution of resources within the farm family along gender lines. It is evident from previous chapters that the weight of culture, tradition, and family ideology in rural Ireland clearly identifies the farm family as a patriarchal structure where the interests of men (fathers and sons) supersede those of women and daughters. Unless farm wives have a separate income source outside of the family farm, they are perceived as dependants of male farmers and are categorised as such in the taxation and social welfare codes. (See Second Commission on the Status of Women Report, 1993, for a detailed discussion).

When a woman marries a farmer she does not receive, as of right, any proprietary entitlement in respect of the farm holding or family home during the couple's lifetime.[1] Only in the event of the death of the landholder is the farm wife legally protected in terms of rights to her husband's estate.[2] This arrangement is indeed ironic – not until after his death is a husband required by law to share his property with his wife, regardless of her input to the family enterprise. Even then, her ownership is usually considered a temporary arrangement until eventual transfer to one of the couple's children. Partnerships, co-ownership or other legal arrangements are comparatively rare among farming families in Ireland.

1. The Family Home Protection Act 1976 provides women with only a right of veto on the sale of the family home.

2. The Succession Act 1965 provides widows with a minimum entitlement to part of the estate.

Indeed, the existence of a tax on the transfer of gifts between spouses until 1990 actually reinforced the tradition of sole ownership and discouraged transfer of the farm to joint ownership.

Clearly, women enter family farming on a different basis from the men that they marry. For the most part they remain in this situation throughout their married life as there is no legal requirement for husbands to share property, capital, or income with them. Unless they have an independent income in their own right, farm wives' access to money and other family assets in this situation can be wholly dependent on the negotiation of a satisfactory sharing arrangement with their husbands. Their bargaining power will be dependent on their status inside the family and the farm as well as on the nature of the conjugal contract. Moreover, their capacity to use the ultimate sanction of leaving the marriage has been constrained by the non-availability of divorce. Since Ireland did not have legal provision for divorce until 1996, marriage has largely been looked upon as a permanent arrangement. This further reduced the options available to women. Ironically, if they do find their position intolerable and seek a legal separation, the Judicial Separation and Family Law Reform Act 1989 provides for a kind of deferred community property. This Act allows the court, when deciding a judicial separation, to order a division of property to take into account, inter alia, the contribution of the wife to the welfare of the family, and the effect on her earning capacity of having taken on marital responsibilities.

The decision to leave a marriage would however also depend very much on the options outside. Farm wives who see little possibility of being able to earn an independent income outside the farm family are more likely to remain within it, even if they feel powerless and subordinated through not being rewarded or recognised for their contribution. Marriage is also much more than just an economic arrangement, so that ideologies of family and of wife/motherhood in family farming will also structure women's action and the way they assess their situation. Indeed the shifts in the ideology of marriage and family in Ireland which as we have noted earlier, have come to stress sharing and mutual obligation, tend to underplay the material aspects of marriage which were much more explicit in the days of the arranged 'match'.

Ownership of Land and Property

Only eighteen percent of all farms in the study were in joint ownership. The majority of these were in the west, where twenty-seven percent

(8/30) of farms were owned jointly by husband and wife. In just three of these cases the transfer to joint names was a deliberate decision taken after marriage. In two of the remaining five farms, the husband had 'married in' to the wife's farm; in two, the farm had been handed over as a gift to the couple at marriage. In the remaining instance the land had been purchased by the couple after marriage. The only case of female sole ownership was that of a woman who had recently been widowed. In the east, a mere ten percent (3/30) of farms were owned jointly by the farm couple – one where the land was acquired after marriage, a second where the husband 'married in' and one where the woman herself purchased the land after marriage (with money which was a gift from her father) and was effectively the farmer. Only in two cases of recent widowhood was the land owned solely by a women.

Joint ownership occurred therefore only in situations where the couple had a strong commitment to sharing as in the three instances in the west, or where land was purchased after marriage. Even on those farms described in Chapter Five where the working relationship indicated a shared commitment to the family farm enterprise, male ownership still prevailed in the majority of cases. The association of ownership with the male 'farmer' and the patrilineal system is so strong that even in cases where the husband 'marries in' to his wife's family farm, the land is invariably put into joint ownership rather than retained solely in her name. Generally though, as long as their husbands are alive, farm women themselves appear unconcerned about the issue of ownership of land even where they are making a very significant labour input to farm production. Their awareness of the possibility of being in a difficult predicament in the event of their husband's death, however, means that having a will made is regarded as an important insurance against future insecurity:

The house and farm are in H's name. . . Sometimes I think about it . . . if something happened, but I would get it anyway as he has a will made. I have my name on the cheque book. That is important, it makes business straightforward. (E7)

The farm is mainly in H's name. There is another piece in both our names and a piece in our son's name. The house is in H's name. It doesn't bother me at all, he won't throw me out! I'd fight my corner. (E10)

The land being in my husband's name doesn't bother me, we have a will made and I am not a feminist. I think feminists draw things on themselves, make a big issue of things; it depends on the family. There are families with big problems. It's easy to get smug when things are going well. (E18)

The land is in H's name. It doesn't bother me, we have our wills made. . . That's why I'm happy enough. (E24)

The house and farm are in H's name but he has a will made, he is very proper like that. I don't mind at all. God between us and all harm, but if he died it is mine. (E27)

Women don't think about their name on the farm, unless a situation crops up, they just drift along. They don't think of these things. I never thought of it myself until a neighbour died suddenly. (W29)

It is apparent that the family farm remains firmly in the hands of husbands, particularly in the east. Ownership of the land there would also embrace other capital assets such as buildings, animals and machinery. Rarely are substantial proportions of such assets assigned separately to the farm wife, although it is not uncommon for various members of the family to own animals, particularly a son who might be a potential successor.

There was little difference between the two areas in relation to ownership of the family home. Overall, forty percent (24/60) of family homes were jointly owned. In the west 43 percent (13/30) of farm homes were owned by the farm couple and in the east the corresponding proportion was 37 percent (11/30). In the west, eight of these homes were on farms which were jointly owned; in one case the home, but not the farm, was in both names. In the remaining four cases the houses had been recently built or renovated. Building a new home was a more common reason for joint ownership in the east where nine out of the eleven jointly owned homes were new. Older houses which were part of the husband's patrimony, or built before his marriage, are more likely to be registered, along with the land, solely in his name.

Most farm women then did not have ownership rights to the land on family farms regardless of their labour or financial input. Joint ownership was the exception and there is little evidence of any significant movement towards a more egalitarian regime. Ownership of land on family farms is structured by gender and the requirements of the patrilineal system of inheritance. Even a widow's ownership of land is regarded as a temporary stage until ultimate transfer to a male successor. Women's apparent unconcern about this may owe as much to a recognition of the impregnability of the system as to anything else, but it may also be rooted in their sense of being an outsider, of 'marrying in' to their husband's family property and therefore not having any 'rights'. Only joint purchase of a farm or their husband's explicit recognition of their contribution can alter the pattern of male dominance. The essentially patriarchal nature of ownership of family property is apparent in the fact that the situation does not appear to hold in reverse. When men 'married in' they became joint owners. The fact that joint ownership was much less common in the east suggests a stronger commitment on the part of male farm owners there to maintaining the gendered structure of ownership on larger, more commercial farms.

The pattern of home ownership indicates a trend towards separation of ownership arrangements, with younger couples building new homes which are jointly owned. The emergence of joint ownership of the home coincides with a shift to more egalitarian ideologies of marriage discussed earlier in Chapter Four, but is also related to farm wives' involvement in paid employment, since wives who were joint owners of new homes were frequently working off the farm. We have already noted how farm wives who are involved in paid work use their income to strengthen their bargaining position and achieve what they consider desirable living standards. There is evidence that this includes the construction of new family homes in joint ownership which reflect the ideological and power shifts discussed in earlier chapters, and also represent a real and symbolic detachment of family from farm, particularly in cases where the farm wives concerned have no significant involvement in the farm operation.

Sources of Income

The pattern of unequal ownership of farm and family assets described above confirms the patriarchal character of family farming in Ireland. However, while unequal distribution of ownership of such assets may impinge on women at points of crisis, or may structure the broad outlines of distribution within the family, gendered work roles assign to women the task of meeting the daily consumption needs of the family. Consequently, constraints on their access to, and control over, money may be a much more proximate source of subordination.

The need to generate income plays a large part in structuring day-to-day family life and has quite a distinct character in self-employed occupations such as farming. This was evident from some of the discussion in earlier chapters, as was the importance of personal money in giving farm women a sense of their own worth. For women engaged in paid work, having an independent income is a conscious source of personal freedom and autonomy. It was also apparent that the way in which money is handled in farm households reflects the character of the working relationship and the conjugal contract between the spouses. More importantly it reveals the ideology of marriage and family which shapes everyday interactions, and the extent to which it embodies the notion of male breadwinner and 'boss', or is characterised by more egalitarian ideas of partnership. It is likely that patterns of allocation of money within the household reflect and reinforce the relative power of the spouses.

Money allocation is a complex issue when the farm household or family is the unit of analysis. Many farm households have multiple sources of income. Not only may either husband or wife engage in full-time, part-time or occasional paid work, but adult family members may be living at home and contributing to the household budget. Likewise, older relatives may be in receipt of pensions and contributing regularly or occasionally. However, to take account of all these possibilities would complicate the analysis unnecessarily and divert attention away from the main issues under consideration. Consequently, only the earning activities of husbands and wives are examined here. These are sum-marised in Table 6.1.

Table 6.1
Sources of Income in Farm Families of Respondents

Income Sources	West		East	
	%	No.	%	No.
Farming only	33	10	43	13
Farming & transfers or social employment/training schemes	17	5	3	1
Husband has non-farm earned income	30	9	17	5
Wife has non-farm earned income	10	3	30	9
Both have non-farm earned income	10	3	7	2
Total	100	30	100	30

Just a third of couples in the west and somewhat more in the east relied solely on farming income. The majority of farm families therefore had more than one source of income. In the west, half the farm couples had some form of earned income.[3] The proportion was higher (54 percent) in the east, mainly due to the greater numbers of wives involved in paid work. Transfer payments, not surprisingly, were an income source on the farms in the west, where small-scale farming predominates.

3. Earned income here does not necessarily refer to full-time employment but to any regular non-farm earned income.

Patterns of Allocation of Money

Given this diversity of income sources, it is not surprising that the ways in which farm families in the present study handled their finances were very much related to the level and sources of their income, and the nature of the conjugal relationship. The fact that income from farming is often irregular and unpredictable determines that, in families where farming is the only source of income, rigid systems of allocation of a fixed amount every week/month are impossible. The clear (but rather static) categories of allocation constructed by Pahl (1989) and Burgoyne (1990) for the UK, and Rottman (1994) for Ireland, are of little relevance here. Where either husband or wife or both are in paid work their income may be less individualised than is the norm in other non-farm households, because of the strong family ideology in farming or because the shift in income balance can, as we have seen in earlier chapters, alter the power relationships between spouses.

Control and Management

There were quite marked differences in the ways that farm wives described how family finances were organised – mainly associated with the level and sources of income. In the west, where incomes were generally lower, farm wives were much more involved in both managing and controlling the family's finances. This careful budgeting in situations of scarcity is consistent with the findings from other studies that women have always played an important material role in low-income families (Brannen and Wilson, 1987; Pahl, 1989; Rottman, 1994). Indeed Wilson (1987: 154) has pointed out that there is a strong ideology of female responsibility for family welfare among low-income women. Rottman (1994: 67) also found that in Ireland wife-managed finances are most common in the poorest households and on farms.

In the west, farm wives' accounts of the way that finances were managed in the largely subsistence farm/household economies of the earlier generation revealed that women there generally controlled the money. On such farms, regular cash income was largely generated by farm women through the farmyard economy of poultry and butter-making, while income from crops and animals was more erratic. Women therefore often controlled what regular money was available, keeping cash in the house to be drawn on when needed. Men handed over the proceeds of the sale of animals and crops to their wives who kept it until it was needed. Many women in the west described their mothers controlling the money in this way:

When I was growing up, my father always gave my mother all the money. He had no money himself. In those days I don't think people used the banks much, the money was kept in the house, maybe that's why the women kept it. (W7)

My mother managed the money in our house. She bought cigarettes for my father but he never had any money. He wouldn't have a penny. I'm not like that but I certainly control it, he gives it to me. (W16)

My father never knew where the money was. My mother controlled it completely. If he was going to the fair, she would have it ready for him in the morning. It was backways it went in the next generation [with the men controlling the money more]. Of course the women had to be good [managers] to control the money. My mother set out all the jobs for the children, father was only brought in for big things and then it was serious. He was the 'quiet man in the corner' but when he spoke, you listened. (W25)

I look after the money here and my mother did also [in our house] but I would say she was much tighter, more careful with money. I suppose she had to be, she didn't have much. (W11)

Although commoditisation, involving a much greater need for the use of cheque books and bank accounts, eventually removed cash from the farm kitchen, this appears to have happened much more slowly in the west (Curtin, 1986). Even in the 1970s Hannan and Katsiaouni found that 38 percent of the western farm families they studied did not use banks but kept money in the house. In nearly half the families they found what appeared to be a 'very casual, uncalculating approach towards money' (1977: 75).

Women on farms in the west continue to insist on control and management of family money as far as possible and are very forthright about the need for women to have this control:

Women wouldn't be so soft as to let husbands have the money. My daughter-in-law for instance – my son hands his wages up to her. If you had to ask husbands for money, they would know the price of everything you bought, even the cost of getting your hair done! (W7)

I do the money management here and keep accounts. We discuss everything and H takes a few bob [for himself]. We have a joint account but it is nearly always me that uses it. I use the money for the running of the house. . . I knew what came in here and never had to account for it. If I wanted to buy an outfit H would never question what I spent on it. He would never ask me what I spent going to town. Life for me would be very difficult if I had that situation. . . Very few women will spend money foolishly. No man is as good a manager with money as a woman. Things would be very different if I had that problem. That's why I never wanted to go out to work. . . Even if I spent

£200 on an outfit H wouldn't even want to know. It is very hard for women who have that problem, you would say I worked all those years and at the end of the day I had nothing. (W9)

I've heard of a case where a woman goes in and does the shopping and the man [her husband] goes in and pays – that's diabolical. My husband would-n't know what was in my purse. You couldn't be full time asking men for money, they don't know the prices, they don't understand. Women have to control it. (W6)

What women mean by control in these instances is comparative freedom to manage and spend the household finances without feeling constrained by husbands' queries or disapproval. However on smaller holdings such control does not usually involve much discretionary spending but requires considerable management skills. Such situations often involve women in the kind of working partnership described in Chapter Five as 'working for the family farm' and are generally found on family farms where money is scarce and there is little surplus for personal spending even where there is some off-farm income. Most expenditure is dictated by basic consumption needs but couples are more likely to decide together on spending priorities. Two-thirds of couples in the west had joint bank accounts, which Pahl (1989) considers to be an important indicator of sharing. Of the remaining third, half had separate accounts for husband and wife and only in seventeen percent of all couples did the husband alone have a bank account.

The Housekeeping Allowance and Feelings of Dependency

The practice of providing an allowance for household expenses was the exception rather than the rule in the west where income scarcity on small holdings predominated. In the east, on the larger, more commer-cial farms, it appeared to be the norm with women's access to 'family income' being much more restricted. Many farm wives (who are not themselves in paid employment) are given a fixed amount for running the house and have only limited access to the remainder of the farm income. Only a third of couples in the east have a joint bank account and there is a much higher incidence of husband and wife having sepa-rate accounts than was found in the west – thirty-seven percent as opposed to seventeen percent. Farm women in this situation think of the allowance as money which they manage, but they do not have control over the family's finances – merely the allowance which they are allo-cated. They see the farm income very much as being their husbands. Each of the women quoted below think of the farm income in this way and in each instance a different strategy has evolved to ensure that wives can have access to extra money. All three are on large commercial farms:

> I get wages [an allowance] for the house but if I wanted anything I get a cheque from H. . . If I need money I'd take it from H's trousers. He wouldn't stop you getting anything, I'm not extravagant. (E1)

> At the beginning we had accounts in the shops so I could get what I needed but I had to ask for money for Mass and things like that. It was not that he wouldn't give it or was mean, it was having to ask. . . I told H that I was clearing off if I was not getting money. He didn't understand, he had his own money and I had none. I don't have this problem any more, I just take it now. I have had my own account for ten years now. Men don't understand this. (E5)

> I get so much every week for the house. I have a charolais bullock every year for myself and he makes about £1,100. I have my own account in my own name. I am very lucky, H will give me money to put into it now and again, if a cheque comes in he might say 'take that for your account in case it is getting a bit low'. (E24)

These women describe an experience of financial dependency which is felt by many farm wives who do not have a personal income through paid work. At best, they may control and spend the family money needed for day-to-day consumption but they still do not look upon it as theirs, even though they may have a personal bank account. Like the women quoted above, they are grateful and consider themselves fortunate to have 'generous' husbands. At worst they have to ask husbands directly for money, rely on Child Benefit, or work out elaborate strategies to access money for personal spending. Many have small 'thrift accounts' on which they can draw in emergencies or in cases of unexpected expense:

> I miss having my own money, although now I have the children's allowance. When I had my own money I spent it on the children and I would still. (E1)

> Now I go to the supermarket and pay in cash. I used to pay by cheque but now I get cash and get more than I need for groceries and keep the rest! (E5)

> I'm saving up the childrens' allowance [Child Benefit] for a [clothes] dryer, or maybe Santa will give it to me. (E8)

> He has to sign the cheque if I want to get out money. I would take the money then and feel free to spend it [some hesitancy here] within reason. Yes I found it hard at the beginning, I was used to having my own wages and I found it hard to share and to spend on myself. I would like to have my own money. (W12)

One farm wife, comparing herself and her married daughter who works as a nurse, captured the difference between them in this way:

> She has her own cheque book and she would be freer with spending money where I'd have to be tighter. She would buy new tea towels whereas I would keep them until they are old . . . things like that. I don't have my own cheque book and I can't sign any cheques. (E20)

Even women who are in a working relationship such as that described earlier as 'working for the family farm' can express a longing for personal money, although it is more unusual among this category:

> I would like to visit my daughter in England but it is difficult to organise. I would hate to go on my own, what would I be doing there without H. I would love to have my own money to save up for these things like holidays. That's when you would like to have your own money. (W5)

Regardless of their access to family resources, women feel acutely the dependency associated with 'not having your own money'. Having no personal money devalues farm wives' domestic work in their own eyes and reinforces their sense of needing to prove that they are 'deserving' or of being grateful for a generous husband. In regard to no other issue did the women's own sense of their subordination and dependency emerge so clearly. Such feelings are not necessarily associated with authoritarian husbands who are explicitly coercive, but in many cases, it reflects rather the influence of very powerful family ideologies which assigns men to the role of breadwinner and women to that of self-sacrificing home manger. It seemed ironic when several interviewees described their mothers as having had a personal income for the first time when they were widowed and commented on how much enjoyment their mothers appeared to derive from 'having their own money and freedom'.

Women's Non-Farm Income and Family Finances

Twenty percent of farm wives in the west and thirty-seven percent in the east had some non-farm earned income (Table 6.1). Having their own income really mitigates women's feeling of dependency and the need to be accountable to their husbands. It allows them to have their own personal bank account, even though they might have a joint account as well. The extent to which their income can be used for discretionary spending however, depends on its significance to family finances. Women may not feel that they have much choice about spending when the extra income becomes more critical as children grow older and more expensive. Both the following respondent and her husband, on a smallholding in the west, have part-time jobs. She explains the need for extra money:

> There are only a few pounds out of the farm, when kids are looking for money you need a weekly wage. I had stamps [Unemployment Benefit] for fifteen months and then had nothing. I really missed the money for extra things for the kids. I am only doing this work now in order to build up the stamps [UB entitlement] so I can sign on when I have nothing. (W16)

In the discussion of the significance of off-farm paid work in the previous chapter, it was clear that women use their off-farm incomes to 'run the house'. This is consistent with Rottman's (1994) finding, from a national sample, that 62 percent of women's income is usually spent on general housekeeping expenses. This income is essential in situations where family finances are under pressure, but women also express a sense of 'ownership' of the money they earn:

> We couldn't live on the farm income, especially with a mortgage. If I had the option I would prefer to work part-time especially when the kids are young. Teaching is hard work but we couldn't do without the money. . . Having my own money is important especially for the kids. Well, it's not my own money but I wouldn't like to have to ask. I have my own account and he has his. We have a joint account and the farm income is separate. I use my own money for running the house, paying the mortgage and for the kids. (Teacher, E15)

> The money I earn is my money. I spend most of it, I get what I want. I claim for the mortgage, pay for it and buy the groceries as well. I would say to H if I wanted more money. I have my own account, H's farm account is separate. We didn't organise anything, I would just get what I want and if I need money I'd ask him. He pays the phone, electricity, car insurance, changes the car and so on – it is joint really. (Nurse, E17)

> H has a farm account and all the money from the farm goes into that. I have my own account and my wages go in there. I pay out of that clothing, the car, the baby-minder and so on. There is nothing left at the end of the day. (Laboratory technician, E22)

Women's expenditure of their own earned incomes has the effect of improving the family's standard of living. There is more money available for the day-to-day consumption needs of the family as well as a higher standard of housing and material possessions. It also gives women a sense of control and influence associated with their sense of ownership of the money spent. More fundamentally, it allows the diversion of farm income, which would otherwise be used for family living expenses, to husbands for further farm investment or accumulation. In each of the three cases above, and in others where either of the couple had a non-farm income, the farm account was kept separately. In the east, half the farms studied had a separate bank account for the farm, while in the west only just over a quarter of farm families (27 percent) had this arrangement. Not surprisingly, these accounts were controlled by husbands. Thus, while the generation of non-farm income can release farm income for much needed investment on smaller holdings (eventually augmenting family income), on larger holdings it may encourage accumulation strategies which facilitate the expansion of patriarchal property ownership, and perhaps accentuate already well-established gender inequalities.

Everyday Consumption

'Putting Myself Last'

Regardless of whether or not they have 'their own' money, women tend to fall to the bottom of the family hierarchy of consumption. As Land has pointed out, the constraints of low income are not equally shared within the family and even though women play a major role in managing household finances, they will put themselves last particularly where money is scarce (1977:174). In the following case – a farm with a market gardening enterprise in the east – the farm wife who has five children, described her control of the family finances in the following way:

> I always handled the money. Before his marriage H's sister handled the money so it was natural that I took over. It was not the same in my house, my father handled the money and gave it to my mother. It was important to me; I am better able to handle scarcity and conceal things and stretch money. As I got older I learned to look for credit and not feel I had to pay for things right away. I always put myself last, I had the same coat for the first four children, a green one with a fur collar. I got a new coat for the fifth and I hung the old one out in the shed. I did without myself and no one ever knew. (E4)

As the children grew up she prepared for a secure future by saving for them:

> I put away money for them every week. They knew I was doing it but they didn't know how much I had. . . When they got married they had a few pounds for mortgages. We divided the place at the marriages and each one

got their own loan for a house with the money I had put aside for a deposit. (E4)

Saving on behalf of children in this way is not uncommon, particularly when they are living at home as wage-earning adults. Mothers often do not take any contribution to household expenses from such resident children or deposit their contribution in a savings account. It is part of the logic of the household economy by which wives/mothers feel guilty about spending money on themselves and is quite independent of whether or not money is scarce, whether women control it, or are themselves in paid work:

> I look on the farm money as joint money and I could spend more if I wanted to. Anything I really wanted I could get but it is easier to buy for others and you are inclined to leave yourself. If I won the Lotto I would give the money away, spread it around. I don't know. I'd put some by for the kids and spend it in moderation. (E10)

> Since I had kids, I've noticed how I head for the babies section in shops, not the ladies – to see if there is anything nice for them. I suppose I feel guilty buying for myself, I think of what they need. I'd put myself last, I'd need to be going somewhere before I would buy anything. (E21)

> I was never without a pay packet really . . . so I always had that independence. I had my own account and I used it for the house and for the babies. I wouldn't feel as free to spend money on myself, women have a built-in guilt complex. I couldn't see anyone going short and me going out and spending money. (E22)

> Money! I often feel where is it going to come from. I wouldn't really feel free to buy things for myself but I'm not into fashion or dressing up. The last decent thing I bought was last October to go to a wedding but I might treat myself to something soon. We don't go places anyway. I would feel guilty spending it, I'd feel less guilty buying milk powder [for the calves]. (E27)

Even though women who are in paid employment are still inclined to put family before themselves, having a personal income does strengthen farm wives' sense of freedom and autonomy. As a respondent who ran her own business commented:

> With your own money you would buy things that you wouldn't otherwise buy for yourself. It is different buying things for yourself. With his money you wouldn't buy as much. (E28)

Another farm wife who has returned to work as a nurse said:

> It's nice not to feel guilty about bills, to buy things, to have a better quality of life. Working enables me to justify buying things, to say 'you work hard so you deserve it'. Having said that, H is not mean and I am reasonable with money. (E29)

However they spend it, women do see earned money as rightfully theirs and earning it allows them to be more assertive. It means that their contribution to the family has a visible value, thus allowing them to value themselves. Moreover, implicitly at least, it also gives them the power of withdrawal of their contribution as a sanction. More fundamentally, being an income earner can provide farm women with an escape from financial dependence in marriage and the family enterprise and a possibility to consider an alternative lifepath should the marriage itself become intolerable.

Women's Autonomy and Access to Transportation

Virtually all of the women interviewed lived in the open countryside where physical access to the wider society is dependent on private transportation. Consequently, being able to drive and having access to a car essentially determines their freedom to move out of the farm home; otherwise they are dependent on someone else to travel any appreciable distance. Being able to drive is regarded as a critically important element of their lives by farm women themselves and is keenly regretted by those unable to do so. In a sense driving, and, in some cases, car ownership have given women a kind of personal freedom which they appreciate greatly and perceive as part of women's advancement. As we shall see, access to a car captures in microcosm many of the issues associated with gendered consumption.

Car ownership in the two areas reflects the differences in incomes and associated material wealth (Table 6.2). Not surprisingly, in the east there are more women who drive and they have more cars available to them. Just over half of all the study households there have two or more cars. More than a third of women in the west did not have a driving licence, even though there was only one household without a car.

Being able to drive and having access to a car allows women to organise the daily routine of their lives without depending on their husbands for transportation as was often the case with their mothers. A mother of four children, all under ten, explains:

> Being able to drive is definitely important. My mother-in-law doesn't drive and it is a disadvantage. My mother learned at sixty as she said she was sick of asking people to drive her places. She has stopped now as she is sev-

enty three. I have been driving since I was seventeen and I have my own car. (E8)

Women who married before they had learned to drive often only realised how dependent their inability to drive had made them when they had to rely on the (sometimes condescending) goodwill of others for transportation:

I started driving out of desperation. I had a licence from before you had to take the test and I just did it because I had to. Otherwise, I had to get H to drive me everywhere. I was very nervous at first and every time H and I went out we would have a row . . . but I couldn't imagine what my life would be like if I didn't drive, it is very important. (E16)

Driving is very important. It would drive me mad not to have a car, you would have no comfort. You can come and go as you please. Once I had to come out of the hairdressers with colour in my hair and my hair wet because I thought H was waiting for me. . . I learned to drive after getting married. One of my daughters hasn't passed her test yet and I am always giving out to her. . . If you couldn't drive you'd be stuck to the four walls. With a car you don't have to be rushing and all that. (E20)

I didn't drive a car until 1972 or 1973, one night when H was so drunk that I had to take over and I have been driving since. I never bothered even though I was driving the tractor for years. As soon as my daughters were seventeen I told them to get a licence. Sometimes I think I would be better if I never started . . . as I had to do so much driving. (E23)

Not being able to drive is a disadvantage. H is always in a hurry. If I could drive, I could go places myself. (W23)

Table 6.2
Car Ownership in Study Households

No. of Cars in Household	West		East	
	%	No.	%	No.
0	3	1	0	0
1	63	19	47	14
2	33	10	43	13
3	0	0	10	3
Total	100	30	100	30
Wives with Driving Licence	63	19	90	27

Those who do not drive usually rely on their husbands or adult children for transportation. Such arrangements curtail and alter the nature of their social interactions. For instance when they go to the shops they are always aware of being a source of delay to their driver and this heightens their sense of dependence. Two of the women from the west explained it in this way:

It's a big disadvantage and it's also hard on H. He has to wait for me when I'm doing the big grocery shopping and it's a nuisance especially if he is busy with hay or anything. Even to go down home when my stepmother was bad [ill], H had to bring me every time. (W2)

I feel bad about not being able to drive the car. I haven't the courage now to learn. It means you can't go anywhere alone without asking a man to take you. The family were always around to take me too so I didn't realise what a disadvantage it was for a while. If H had kept the small car that we had I might have considered trying to learn, but he got a few hundred for it and he sold it. Now we have a big diesel and I would be afraid to drive it. If H had kept the old one, I was thinking I could go to Galway and visit my family. My daughter just passed her test. She failed it the first time and I was always on to her to keep up the driving as it's such a setback not to be able to. When she was home we had a great time going around. (W5)

In this case the husband's disposal of the 'small car' effectively precluded his wife from considering the possibility of learning to drive. The large car is effectively his property and responsibility. She can only resist by ensuring that her daughter does not suffer the same fate, as in the case quoted earlier. This was a point which other non-drivers repeatedly emphasised.

Even when farm wives have a driving licence, access to the 'family car' is often difficult, requiring negotiation with husbands who see themselves as having first claim on it as a part of the family enterprise:

There was a problem with the family car, I could never get it as he always wanted it or was in a hurry to get it back. . . It was terrible not to be able to go anywhere, to be always tied to time or to be somewhere and have someone waiting for you. There wasn't much sharing of the car here it was all a one-sided affair. The land is scattered so the car was needed. (W24)

This woman now shares a car with her sister and is relieved that she no longer has to negotiate with her husband. Indeed husbands sometimes discourage wives wishing to learn to drive by telling them they are not 'mechanically minded', or by criticising them when they have had a minor accident. While several cases of women learning to drive in their fifties and sixties were instanced, it was almost always in cases of widowhood or husbands' incapacitating illnesses. In other words women had to learn, as they described it, out of 'sheer necessity'.

Not surprisingly, women who have managed to acquire their own cars have a strong sense of the significance of this in their lives:

> I am driving since I was seventeen; my mother learned when she was fifty! Not being able to drive doesn't bear thinking about. . . I would feel isolated. (W1)

> I have my own car, it is very important. I'd be really handicapped if I had no car. I couldn't go, say, with the kids to school. When I need a car H could be out at the other end of the farm with the car. (W17)

In a sense then the whole issue of car ownership, driving, and access to the family car captures in microcosm the way in which inequalities within the family are structured on the basis of gender. Women's access to a car, while influenced in the broadest sense by economic considerations (whether the family or the individual woman can afford a car), is influenced more proximately by their husbands' control of this family asset and the degree to which they are considered to have a legitimate right to use it. Women clearly recognise this and have become more assertive in claiming the 'family' car. This in turn can result in taking on a range of family errands which may reinforce their status of helper. On balance however, it creates a sense of personal freedom and autonomy which was unavailable to their mothers. Indeed some mothers have learned to drive when they were widowed 'out of necessity' and now enjoy what they consider a new freedom and mobility.

Women and Consumption – Some Conclusions

Women in farm families find themselves in a collectivity which is suffused with ideologies of patriarchal family farming on the one hand, and of sharing and family solidarity on the other. The fact that comparatively few women have ownership rights to the family farm indicates that there is little breaching of male dominance over ownership of the means of production. The assumption of sharing within the farm family is so strong that asymmetry of ownership is legally unacceptable only when the marriage is severed through death or separation. Even then, widows are perceived as having a caretaker role until a son can take over. This was the case in each situation of widowhood in the study. However, women themselves are not particularly concerned about the issue of ownership, perhaps because it is a relatively remote matter. Much more important and proximate sources of subordination, in their accounts, are their access to and control over money, or whether they can drive the family car (or their own car) when they wish.

Farm women's involvement in paid work may, ironically, have the effect of reinforcing men's control over family assets, particularly on larger more commercial holdings since farm profits can be diverted away from domestic expenditure and reinvested in the farm. Thus, women's earning power is often critical in allowing the farm to develop commercially – an achievement which is usually attributed to the skill and resourcefulness of the male farmer. Women are beginning to make some inroads into joint ownership of the family home but often only because their earnings are material to its acquisition and maintenance. In this way they provide a higher material standard of living for the whole family.

In regard to day-to-day consumption, women assume greater control over family income and expenditure in circumstances of low income and scarcity – a situation which is consistent with findings from other studies. Consequently, in the west where low incomes were more prevalent, there was much greater evidence of sharing the burdens associated with irregular and inadequate income in much the same way as described earlier as characterising some farm families' work regimes. In the east, women's own involvement in paid work and the practice of a household budget allowance system means that financial arrangements there take on a different character. There is much more separation between farm and home so that accumulation strategies reinforce women's exclusion from ownership of farm assets. In the west, where little accumulation is possible, there is much more sharing.

The issue of access to a car captures in microcosm, women's day-to-day experiences of dependency and how they can be exaggerated or mitigated by the availability of transportation. It is through these everyday experiences of differential access to consumption goods, taken for granted as being available to men, that women's subordination is maintained and reinforced. Not surprisingly, farm women urge their daughters to avoid the obvious pitfalls of such dependency. Like women everywhere, farm women, regardless of their access to money, will put themselves last on the family consumption hierarchy. The fact of farming being a family enterprise probably accentuates this tendency. A large part of farm women's lives is devoted to securely establishing the next generation, whether in or outside the family enterprise. It is women's involvement in this process of constructing the future that is the subject of the next chapter.

7

SECURING THE FUTURE

The Reproductive Role of Farm Women

Introduction – Understanding Reproduction

In the preceding three chapters we have elaborated women's experiences of family farming by exploring their entry into family farming via marriage, their work roles, and their access to farm family resources. Much of what emerged has confirmed that women are constrained by patriarchal structures of control, but the ways in which women 'fight back', how they contest and negotiate patriarchy, and some of the sources of their empowerment also became apparent. In this context there was evidence of the way in which the actions of farm women shape the future, in so far as their day-to-day influence on the family farm extends, not just to production and consumption, but beyond biological reproduction to the whole process of re-creation of social life by which society is perpetuated. It is to the sphere of reproduction that we now turn and, in so doing, attempt to broaden the focus of investigation to explore farm women's direct influence on the future of family farming and the wider social formation.

The problems and ambiguities surrounding the concept of reproduction in family farming have already been discussed in Chapter Two. The concept of reproduction is central to analyses of simple commodity production and the evolution of family farming, but is couched in such general terms that it is difficult to discern how the internal relations of the family farm affect reproduction. Van der Ploeg (1986) has attempted to explain reproduction as the transformation of social relations within the commoditisation process by distinguishing between market-dependent and autonomous reproduction. This does not, however, take us any closer to understanding how social relations within farm families or social actors themselves affect reproduction. Whatmore proposes a composite concept of reproduction, in which production and reproduction are linked by the social organisation of labour, so that they are interlocking processes structured by gender and class relations (1991: 40). This brings us nearer to establishing how women actually influence reproduction (apart from in the obvious biological sense of procreation), but Whatmore's emphasis on the labour process restricts her capacity to see women as agents actively constructing the future. Delphy and Leonard (1992), while rejecting feminist usage of the concept of reproduction as confining women's work to a non-economic, non-productive sphere, nevertheless go on themselves to use the concept in a very restrictive way by equating it with inter-generational transmission of the family enterprise.

The critical issue then is to come to an understanding of how family dynamics, which are structured by gender, affect reproduction. First it is necessary to reiterate our understanding of the concept of reproduction. In Chapter Two it was argued that, aside from the biological dimension, there are three basic aspects to reproduction: reproduction of the family farm as a business; reproduction of family farming as a social form; and social reproduction in the wider sense of the re-creation of social life. The first of these essentially involves the reproduction of the farm as a business enterprise, which is a primary source of livelihood for the farm family. We have already explored some of the sources of women's influence in this regard, such as their importance as suppliers of labour to the enterprise, or how their earnings from off-farm work or their skilful management of consumption may release farm income for reinvestment in the farm business. Equally, we have seen how women's actions can affect the evolution of family farming as a social form through, for instance, their determination to work off the farm themselves. We have examined how farm daughters' actions have had a lasting impact on the rural social structure, but farm women's influence on the wider social formation, through their role as mothers, has been dealt with less explicitly up to now. In this chapter we explore farm women's more direct involvement in, and influence on, reproduction through their actions as mothers. Although family is a defining characteristic of the family farm, and inter-generational succession is integral to its continuity, the farm family, like all families, has as one of its central goals the successful establishment of the next generation, either on or off the farm. The organisation of family life on the basis of gender-specific work roles means that farm women who are also mothers (all but one in the present study), have responsibility for child-rearing, socialisation and schooling. They are, therefore, at the centre of this process (i.e., of establishing the next generation). In this chapter we will demonstrate that it is as mothers, more than as wives, that farm women have a profound influence, not just on the future of the farm business and on family farming as a social form, but on the evolution of the Irish class structure generally.

Reproduction as an active process involves shaping the future, and while structuralist explanations of the evolution of Irish society and of the restructuring in Irish agriculture have been common, there have been relatively few attempts to understand how individuals, groups or classes purposefully construct the future. In their analysis of the significance of small-scale landholders in Ireland's socio-economic transformation, Hannan and Commins (1992) have used the concept of 'survival strategies' to show how farmers as a social group have been particularly adept at securing scarce employment opportunities for themselves and their children over the past two decades. They have associated educational achievement, among the children of smallholders in particular, with the high motivation among this class to seek secure off-farm employment for non-inheriting children. Education and examination success were seen by them as avenues to employment in the public service and the professions (1992: 96). Although they identify farm parents as strategic planners who recognise the significance of education in the achievement of occupational status, and plot the future for their children by carefully appraising the available employment opportunities, Hannan and Commins explain the relative success of smallholder's children (compared to the working class in particular) in availing of education and job opportunities as the legacy of a peasant culture and the requirements of the stem family system. Building on Hannan's earlier work, they argue that the most notable feature of the particular form of peasant economy, culture, and social structure which prevailed in the west of Ireland up to the 1960s was its effective survival and reproduction strategy, incorporating efficient arrangements for the dispersal of non-inheriting children. Farm families' success in education and employment, they argue, has its roots in this system and the inherent imperative to find 'places' for non-inheriting children. This explanation is based on the assumption of patriarchal dominance and takes no account of intra-family processes. It is essentially a male-centred view of social reproduction in which Hannan and Commins are quite explicit in referring to the 'survival strategies of individual farm owners', presumably male (1992: 81). Moreover, it is not clear what distinguishes smallholders in this respect, since the stem family system presumably requires efficient dispersal regardless of farm size. Unfortunately we know little about the arrangements which families on larger holdings made for their children in the past. It is probable that parents on 'substantial farms' in all regions, and especially the east and south, had more opportunities for placing their non-inheriting offspring in secure employment, since they owned more capital, and had access to more employment opportunities in local market towns, as well as better links to business.

In fact, as will be shown here, farm women are the key architects of farm families' efforts to secure for their children desirable occupations outside of farming and there are important differences between east and west in this regard. The primacy of the long-standing power of fathers in deciding the fate of children through designation of an heir to the farm has, on smaller holdings at least, been supplanted by the importance of optimising educational opportunity as the means of securing an occupational position – a domain in which women have the greater influence. On larger farms, where inter-generational succession to full-time farming is likely, mothers are contesting fathers' insistence on the heir's full-time occupational apprenticeship on the farm at the expense of education beyond the statutory school-leaving age. This has important implications for the reproduction of family farming as a social form and for the wider class structure. Before turning to a discussion of how the exceptional educational participation of farm children can be interpreted, it is important to set it out in more detail.

Farm Children's Exceptional Educational Achievements

Ireland's occupational structure has changed dramatically over the past three decades. One of the features of the transformation has been what Breen et al. have referred to as the 'rapid growth in credentialism and in the formalisation of the labour market'(1990: 139). From the 1960s onwards growth in the labour market involved the creation of positions associated with industrialisation and economic expansion, while self-employment and unskilled manual jobs declined. In common with other industrialised countries, the Irish labour force has become increasingly specialised and segmented, and employee positions predominate. Recruitment is based largely on educational credentials and, not surprisingly, prospects for occupational mobility are also strongly related to educational achievement (Whelan et al., 1992).

Participation in post-primary education has increased markedly over recent decades following the introduction of free secondary education in 1967. A sharp rise in the numbers remaining in school after the compulsory age of fourteen was particularly noticeable among farm children. In the period 1961 to 1971 the participation rate (the proportion of children in the relevant cohort) for farm children aged 14 to 19 in full-time education rose from 28 percent to 55 percent. This was higher than the average for other social groups and was exceeded only by the children of professionals, employers, and managers (Rottman et al., 1982). Over the 1980 to 1982 period, more than two-thirds of farm children completed the Leaving Certificate compared to only 38 percent of the offspring of semi/skilled manual workers (Breen, 1984). These high levels for all farm children did mask considerable variation within the farm population (see Hannan, 1970; Conway and O'Hara, 1986), but by the end of the 1980s this too had greatly lessened. Hannan and Commins have shown that by 1988-1989 almost three quarters of farm children (73 percent) completed the Leaving Certificate and nearly one-third (31 percent) went on to third level – rates only exceeded by the offspring of those in the highest social group.[1] Two thirds of children from smaller farms of less than fifty acres completed the Leaving Certificate and one-fifth went on to third level. Even on the smallest holdings therefore, farm children have been particularly adept at securing educational credentials. Hannan and Commins have argued that, as a result, working-class children's upward mobility was significantly constrained (1992: 95). In 1992, 88 percent of farm children completed the Leaving Certificate and these rates were again exceeded only by the children of professionals, managers and salaried employees (Higher Education Authority, 1995).

The achievements of farm children are even more striking when we look at their participation in third-level education. In studies of new entrants to higher education, Clancy (1988, 1995) found that farm children were significantly over-represented. In his most recent survey of those who entered third-level education in 1992, he found that 17 percent of entrants came from the social group 'farmers', even though they constituted only 12 percent of the relevant age cohort. The participation ratio[2] of farm children increased markedly during the 1980s from 1.04 in 1980 to 1.35 in 1992 (dropping slightly from 1.45 in 1986). In 1992 an estimated 49 percent of farm children went on to full-time higher education, more than double the percentage in 1980.

1. Hannan and Commins divide the non-farm population into four social groups - upper and intermediate non-manual; other non-manual; skilled manual; semi-skilled manual and unskilled manual.

2. This ratio is an approximate measure of the degree to which each social group is over, under, or proportionately represented among third level-entrants. A participation ratio of 1.00 would mean that the participation of children from the social group in question was in exact proportion to their representation in the population aged under fifteen in the 1986 Census of Population (see Clancy, 1995).

As regards the type of college attended, farm children have had some interesting patterns of participation. Of all those who entered universities in Ireland in 1992 farm children had a participation rate of 1.33 which was lower than that of children of professionals, employers and managers and salaried employees but higher than all other categories. The children of 'other non-manual' and 'semi-skilled manual' workers had participation rates of 0.53 and 0.55 respectively. The nine Regional Technical Colleges established during the 1970s provided important access opportunities for farm children, where by 1986 they comprised 28 percent of entrants with a participation rate of 2.24, the highest of any social group. By 1992 the proportion had dropped back to 22 percent but farm children still had the highest participation ratio of 1.84 (Clancy, 1988, 1995).

Farm families have therefore been very assiduous users of the educational system at both second and third level. Farm children are significantly over-represented in the third-level sector, having made considerable gains relative to other social groups during the 1980s. A major factor in facilitating farm children to achieve such high levels of education has been their entitlement and willingness to utilise the various forms of financial aid to third-level students. More than three-quarters (77 percent) of farm children in higher education had financial aid in 1992 of which 40 percent were in receipt of a Local Authority grant, a higher proportion than in any other socio-economic group. Only among the children of unskilled manual workers was there a higher proportion of third-level students (87 percent) in receipt of financial aid (Clancy, 1995). It seems that farm families, accustomed to dealing with eligibility criteria, form-filling and other bureaucratic procedures associated with EU and state aid to farming, have been quick to grasp the opportunities which state grants for third-level education, and latterly the EU Social Fund, afforded their children. In a multivariate analysis of factors related to varying county admission rates, Clancy (1995: 131–32) found that the proportion of the population engaged in farming proved to be a very important predictor of admission rates to university. Counties with a high proportion of the population engaged in farming had high rates of admission to university.

Gender Differences in Educational Participation

In general, while more girls than boys sit the Leaving Certificate each year, fewer girls go on to third level. Clancy (1995) found that 49 percent of all new entrants to third level colleges in 1992 were female but that gender differences in participation were related to socio-economic background. Again, farm children were exceptional in that farm daughters had a significantly higher participation ratio (1.54) than sons (1.28). Only in two other social groups (other non-manual and semi-skilled manual) did girls have a higher ratio than boys and the gender differences in these categories were very slight. Farm daughters are unique therefore in the sense that, compared with any other social group, far more of them go to college than their brothers. In 1992 almost a fifth (19 percent) of all new female entrants to third level were farm daughters. Close to one-third of the entrants to the female dominated.[3] Colleges of Education were farm children. These gender differences were also apparent in Hannan and O'Riain's (1993) study of young adults who left school in the early 1980s. Their analysis revealed that, in terms of educational attainment, farm daughters were exceptional. Their educational achievement is in turn associated with labour market success and avoidance of unemployment so that they make, in Hannan and O'Riain's terms 'successful transitions to adulthood'(1993: 128).

It is clear that farm families make exceptional efforts to educate their daughters. This has already been referred to in Chapter Four and was associated there with parents' and daughters' wish to maximise their occupational opportunities, since they would never inherit the farm, except by default. What Hannan (1979) referred to as the 'efficient dispersal system' among peasant farmers in the west was particularly effective in the case of farm daughters who have long demonstrated their wish to escape rural areas which offered few opportunities and to avoid the patriarchal structures of Irish family farming. Education was an important avenue of escape for farm daughters in order to secure their future outside of farming and outside of rural areas where employment prospects were often non-existent. Ensuring that daughters have a good education represents, as we shall see below, a conscious strategy on the part of mothers and daughters to enhance the daughters' life chances by enabling them to be financially independent regardless of whether or not they marry a farmer. Education assumes greater urgency in the west where limited local employment opportunities and low farm incomes are more common.

Given the patterns of participation discussed in Chapter Four and those noted above, it is not surprising that women who did marry farmers had lower levels of educational attainment; we have already discussed how farm wives in the present study have relatively low levels of education, particularly in the west. Nevertheless, the gender differences noted

---

3. In 1992, 90 percent of new entrants to Colleges of Education were female.

above are again reflected in the fact that farm wives had much higher levels of education than their husbands. In fact the gender differences in educational attainment among the farm couples are quite striking. In the west 57 percent (17/30) of husbands had no post-primary education, compared to 37 percent (11/30) of wives. Only 13 percent (4/30) had completed the Leaving Certificate or higher compared to 37 percent (11/30) of wives. In the east the gender differences were equally stark. Only one farm wife had no post-primary education, but 43 percent (13/30) of husbands had not gone on to second level. Sixty percent of wives had completed the Leaving Certificate or higher compared to 23 percent (7/30) of husbands. Although farm wives in the west have lower levels of attainment, it will become apparent that the value currently placed on education in the west appears to be greater; women's consciousness of opportunities missed is now one of the factors which impels them to ensure that their daughters have a good education.

Wives then, have higher levels of education than husbands, and levels for both are higher in the east. These patterns are not unexpected as levels of educational attainment among male farmers have traditionally been very low, with the lowest levels on the smallest farms (ACOT, 1981). This was associated with the tendency for inheriting sons to drop out of school at an early age because their labour was needed on the farm, particularly when in many cases their fathers, having married relatively late, were ageing. Since the inheriting son's occupational future was regarded as secure through succession to the farm, continuing in school as a path to eventual employment was considered unnecessary. Thus, compared both to other occupational groups and to their own siblings, farmers have consistently been found to have low levels of educational participation. In this context it is worth noting that when the educational and training programme leading to a vocational qualification in farming (Certificate in Farming) was established in Ireland in 1983, the provision of attractive incentives led to a dramatic improvement in the hitherto very low participation rates of young (aspiring) male farmers in agricultural education and training. Since then, eligibility for certain tax exemptions and EU and state aid to young farmers have been made conditional on possession of the Certificate in Farming and consequently participation rates have remained high.

Given the range of issues raised in this section and the preceding one, there are two points which are worth reiterating here before turning to the farm families in the present study. Firstly, studies of educational participation at both second and third level in Ireland have shown that farm children have been among the highest attainers. They have used the educational system more extensively than virtually any other social group and have benefited significantly from the financial aid provided to third-level students. Secondly, farm daughters are exceptional in that far more of them than their brothers complete second level; in third level, they outnumber farm sons and females from any other social group.

Education – The Domain of Mothers

Within farm households it is mothers who assume the major responsibility for the education of farm children. This is an integral part of the caring and socialisation role which is a major constituent of motherhood in Ireland and elsewhere. It includes all the tasks associated with care and sustenance of school-going children but also involves making key decisions in relation to education. Farm women's monopoly of action and influence in this sphere is reinforced and legitimised by the fact that they generally have more schooling than their husbands, although they may have considerably less than their own or their husband's siblings. It is a critical aspect of the mother role in which they can exert real and lasting influence on social reproduction by ensuring that their children are prepared to exploit occupational opportunities. The means by which mothers exercise their influence range from decisions about what schools children attend, to supervision of homework, attendance at school meetings, as well as constantly encouraging, promoting and reinforcing the value of a good education. They articulate their commitment to education in terms of a conviction that achieving as high a level of attainment as possible is the key to a secure future and to maximising life chances:

> I believe that education is very important, you could never put enough money into children's education. (W15)

> I'd like them to have as much education as possible and go to third level if they were able and interested. (W30)

> Life has changed since I was a child and education has become much more important. They have to make it on their own now with education. (E25)

The educational domain is one in which women perceive clearly that they as mothers, rather than the fathers, have the major influence. They attribute this to the fact that they have a greater appreciation of the value of education, perhaps because they realise that they missed out on it themselves, and they are willing and available to help at lessons as their work is centred around the house and yard. Their husbands, on the other hand, may have relatively little schooling themselves, in many cases having commenced their occupational apprenticeship on the farm by dropping out of school before or during second-level education. This may have been, as suggested earlier, because becoming a 'farmer' by taking over the family holding meant that further educational achievement was considered unnecessary, or because the son who demonstrated the least academic ability was given the farm. At any rate, fathers are inclined to shy away from involvement in school activities:

> Women are more education conscious, I don't know why. Men should know how important it is. (E11)

> It is the women who really appreciate the value of an education. (E5)

> I was the one who kept them at their lessons and looked after the schooling. He wouldn't have a clue. (W13)

> The mother is the one in the house. My husband is out all day, he is only here for meals so I am the one watching them. Education is important for kids today, there are a lot of pressures on kids, only the best will get there. I never went to secondary school and I regret it, it was a shame. (W18)

> I am more fussy about education, H wouldn't be as bothered . . . you must educate children to work. (E17)

In practice, ensuring that their children have the best possible opportunities involves a high degree of personal commitment, household organisation, and care and encouragement on the part of mothers, particularly at crucial times such as during examinations:

> I was the one that kept them at the books and drove them to school in T. which was thirty-two miles morning and evening because I thought it was a better school. And it worked, they will get their ambitions. Where there is a will there is a way. I kept them at the lessons with the back-up of H of course. I make the rules and they follow! (E18)

> I used to stay up with the kids when they were studying and give them a bit of moral support, especially when they were doing exams. They need special care when they are doing exams – to be humoured and to have their meals ready when they come home. (W9)

> There was always an emphasis here on education. We got rid of the TV, it was taking over and now we only rent one at Christmas. I have noticed that since we have no TV they read a lot more. (E6)

> I was the one who kept them at their books, H was gone a lot of the time. (W11)

Things are hectic here since the kids got older, with them and their friends coming and going, exams and points, football teams and so on. (W18)

Over and over again women stressed the importance of education and their commitment to ensuring that their children had every opportunity. They saw themselves as the creators of an environment in which education was very highly valued. This was particularly marked in the west where the scarcity of both family capital and local employment opportunity has always underlined the need for educational credentials. As one respondent put it:

Education is extremely important, it had to be here [in the west]. Education was not taken lightly and of course the [free] transport was mighty. (W11)

Another mother in the west has four children, all of whom went through third level education. All are now in well-paid professional occupations, three of them outside Ireland. She explained her involvement:

I was the one who kept them at their lessons, and went to the school. Both of us have a strong interest in education as we only went to national [primary] school ourselves. . . There was no question of them not doing the Leaving [Certificate]. We were very lucky to be near the school and they were good students . . . they all just knew what they wanted. (W5)

The Cost of Education

There are considerable financial pressures and sacrifices associated with putting children through third-level education, particularly on the low-income holdings in the west. In such circumstances grants and scholarships are very important. On a farm of less than thirty hectares of poor land in the west where the family of three sons had each studied engineering at university level, their mother explained:

We got grants for the three of them but we had a job to get it for the last one. . . He got it eventually though, otherwise he would have had to go to the RTC [Regional Technical College]. . . I kept them at their lessons, they didn't get away at night. There were no discos during school times. We kept them at it although H would be more lenient than me about this. We haven't the money for going out anyway, it was enough to dress them. (W20)

Scarcity of resources seems to strengthen the resolve of both parents and children, who are aware of the hard work and sacrifices involved and have few of the distractions from homework more typical of town and cities. Where big families have to be educated, the older children help out with the younger ones. In the following case there were seven children on a farm of just twenty hectares. At the time of interview five had completed various third-level education courses and were now employed (two in London); one was studying in a Regional Technical College and the youngest was in secondary school. The father of the family had an off-farm job when the children were younger 'to make ends meet'; the mother made the following comment:

> They never caused us any trouble. I was never that anxious for education for myself, my mother wanted me to stay at home with her. But education was very important for both of us for the kids. There was no question that they wouldn't have a career. . . They all helped out and all got grants to go to college. . . They have all been very good here helping each other out and helping us out if we are short – not big amounts, because they don't have it themselves and they need to be saving too. The older ones buy clothes for the younger ones and tide them over if they are stuck. (W9)

Even with the availability of grants, off-farm income is usually an essential component of the drive to educate, especially on smallholdings in the west. This can happen in two ways. Either parent may take up off-farm work to offset the financial demands associated with putting children through school. The income from a parent's relatively unskilled work may be critical to financing a child's third-level education. Alternatively, when the off-farm job is the primary income source, the farm itself may be looked on as a means of funding education:

> Every penny goes back into the farm to build it up. I hope in the long term to have money out of it for the kids' education as we won't get grants. (W19)

Dairying is the most profitable farm enterprise, providing a predictable and regular income to meet the cost of third-level education. It almost always involves a very significant labour input on the part of farm wives. The family mentioned above who had educated their three sons as engineers were dairy farmers. The mother regarded dairying as a vital source of regular income when children are being educated. However, she expects that they will reduce the (labour) intensity of their farm operation when this has been achieved, perhaps by selling the dairy quota and switching to a beef-cow system. In this sense dairy farming is a means to an end, financing the education of children who will almost certainly not continue the enterprise on the smaller dairy farms when their parents retire. Parents who optimise their farm income by developing and operating a dairy system in this way will often switch to a less intensive system once the education costs have been met and it becomes clear that none of their children are interested in dairy farming as an occupation. In one such family the couple had recently sold their milk quota, changing to a less labour intensive beef-cow farming system. The farm wife explained their decision:

> We were encouraged by the kids. Why hold the quota, they said when we will never come back to dairying. So we made the decision. There was not much point in holding on to it. It was better for us and we are glad now because the price has dropped since we sold. . . Life is much simpler now, I think it was getting H down, the seven day week and everything. (W5)

Accepting that the consequence of educational attainment may be disengagement from (dairy) farming for the next generation is not without regret even on the part of mothers who, after all, may have invested decades of labour in the enterprise. They realise, however, that the expectations that education brings may result in children not wishing to continue with farming even where there is a good living to be made. On another dairy farm where the five children aged between twenty and five years are already in, or expected to go to third level, their mother seemed prepared to accept the inevitability of this when she said:

> Having someone to take over the farm is important to us, we are getting old, we would like to see someone taking over. If they don't want to though we can't push them, they would only blame us later. (W18)

Regional Comparisons

It is evident so far that the commitment to educational attainment is particularly marked in the west, and also more challenging, because farming there is generally smaller in scale and less intensive, and the opportunities for off-farm work are limited. The value placed on education by parents in the west, and already articulated in some of the earlier statements and examples in this chapter, was underlined by the farm women interviewed in the study who are themselves teachers:

> Education was always important in the west of Ireland, it was their only hope of salvation. I think it is the women who look after education in the home – they are the ones who come to the school, to parent-teacher meetings. Of course, if the meetings are held during the day, the men can't usually come but even when they are held at night, about eighty-five percent of those

attending are women. When parents come to the school, it's always the women. (Teacher, W29)

A teacher in the east, whose parents were among a group of farmers who had migrated from the west as part of a government land-resettlement scheme, explained the commitment to education there as follows:

Education was very important to my parents . . . it was a priority with both of them. . . I see this different attitude to education myself in school, in the children whose parents, or even grandparents, came from the west. The teachers from the west see it too, a different attitude to education. They say that the people around here got it handy, whereas nothing was handed to you in the west so they had that drive for education. You can see it at parent-teacher meetings too. The kids are very ambitious and want streaming and the parents are very interested. . . At the parent-teacher meeting it is ninety-five percent mothers . . . it is the mother who generally drives the children. (Teacher, E15)

The commitment to educational attainment on smallholdings in the west, which is orchestrated chiefly by women, extends nowadays not just to daughters and non-inheriting sons but to all the children. Farm women there recognise that they themselves and their husbands are from the last generation of adults in full-time farming for whom education was not considered an occupational requirement. Indeed, their siblings in occupations outside farming, whose educational attainment was often considerably higher than their own, may now be important role models for the present generation of farm children. In this sense, the emphasis on educational attainment also represents a lack of faith in the future of farming as an occupation. Full-time farming is not seen as a viable occupational option for the next generation. The best that can be hoped for is that one of the children will find a job sufficiently close to home to farm the holding on a part-time basis. On the larger holdings in the east, on the other hand, there is an expectation that succession to full-time farming will be a viable option for at least one of the present generation. Indeed one or more children may already have commenced their occupational apprenticeship or taken over management. On 40 percent (12/30) of farms in the east, one or more members of the younger generation were involved full-time in farming (either having taken over management, or working with parents) compared to only one such situation in the west. However, mothers were not always wholehearted in their endorsement of children's succession to farming as we shall see in the next section.

Commitment to Education as a Strategy of Resistance

Mothers' commitment to education for their children can be interpreted as a strategy of resistance to their own subordination within family farming and to farming as an occupation. In the case of daughters, it represents an attempt to widen the opportunity set beyond the confines of the wife/mother role so that daughters may achieve a degree of financial independence unavailable to mothers themselves. At the micro level of the family farm, mothers have adopted and shaped new ideologies which challenge the cultural norms which constrain women. They see themselves as the last generation willing to accede to such an extent to the demands of family and farm and they have resolved to secure their daughters' future through ensuring that by having a 'career' they will never be financially dependent:

> It is a very good thing that women have their own careers and have their independence, I think that is very important. Otherwise there is a loss of education and brainpower. . . I would expect my daughter to keep on her career after marriage and children. (W1)

> I'd advise my daughter to keep on her job after marriage for the income and getting out and about and mixing with people. . . It depends on the job too, if it is a routine job . . . but if you are a professional it is different. (W5)

> My daughters don't intend to have big families. The girls will keep on their jobs. (W9)

Mothers, aware that they themselves are the primary proponents of the value of education, believe that appreciation of, and commitment to, educational attainment is itself related to gender. Girls, they argue, are more appreciative of the importance of education and are ambitious for themselves:

> I'm very concerned about education. The boys all left school as soon as they could, I couldn't keep them in school. The girls will do the Leaving [Certificate]. Girls are more ambitious. If you don't go to school, how are you going to get a good job [I say to them]. (W7)

> It's easier to get through to girls, they mature quicker. The boys are not academic but they know they will have to do the Leaving [Certificate]. (W12)

Daughters present during interviews confirmed these views, stressing the importance for women of having their own incomes and independence – views, as noted in Chapters Four and Five, articulated by women respondents working off the farm, who are of course important role models. The level of educational attainment achieved by daughters also bears out these aspirations and mothers express great pride in their daughters' achievements, particularly when they have been attained in traditionally male-dominated occupations.

Commitment to education for sons is associated with disenchantment with farming as an occupation and the risks associated with it. On smaller holdings there is universal acceptance that full-time farming is not an option for the future. All children are encouraged to maximise their educational attainment and selection of an heir is frequently postponed until one of the farm children has secured off-farm employment sufficiently close to the farm to make part-time farming feasible. Indeed, it is accepted by mothers that the cost of educational success of children may be their eventual rejection of farming as an occupation, even on a part-time basis:

> I wouldn't care about selling it [the farm] if the kids had no interest and I don't think H would either. Keeping it in the family name is not important. In the past they wanted the same first name too. I think that is stupid, I don't believe in it at all. (W2)

> It wouldn't bother me if the farm went. I think that H too would rather that the kids had careers. (W19)

> To carry on the name would be nice but it's not important if they were not interested. . . I'd like to see them getting an education. (W30)

Mothers' insistence on occupational options for sons is not usually contested by fathers on these smaller holdings because they have accepted the inevitability of future part-time farming. Nevertheless it is easier for women to orchestrate a future in which there may be no obvious heir to the farm because they are less emotionally attached to the land itself since in most cases the land is their husband's patrimony:

> I'd be different. He is more attached to the land. I suppose it is because it is his family's land. (W27)

> Land is not as important to people as before. There are no young fellows in farming around here. (W30)

Much of the power of fathers in farm families was based on their right to decide on the heir to the patrimony and the provision of an occupational apprenticeship to the selected successor. This power has been greatly eroded and, on smaller farms, fathers have had to recognise that they are the last generation of full-time farmers. In a situation where reproduction of the family farm will now at best be on a part-time basis, securing a local occupation is a more likely determinant of which child will succeed to the patrimony.

Even on larger more commercial farms in the east, where succession is taken for granted and there is an expectation of full-time farming for the next generation, women perceive farming as a difficult and risk-laden occupation. The families in this study were interviewed at a time when many were experiencing a drop in farm incomes. The future of farming was perceived by them as being very uncertain due to reform of the EU Common Agricultural Policy. Farming was also considered to be a very stressful occupation so that women regarded it as important that potential successors have another occupational option as well as farming:

I insisted on my son doing the Leaving Certificate [before staying at home on the farm] and he got five honours. Education is no great load and they need to be educated nowadays. I feel this more strongly than H. We now have two in third level. (E10)

I think it is important to have a professional qualification. I wouldn't like a child to be a full-time farmer, either son or daughter. Carrying on the name is not important to me but it is to H. The name is important; there is some-thing primitive about 'the name'. . . H is realistic, he doesn't expect sacrifices [from his children]. It is no harm in having an education, I'd like to see them have that option. (E15)

In these circumstances there may be conflict between spouses over the schooling of the potential successor. Fathers who have not themselves completed second-level education perceive the inheriting son's continu-ing on in school as delaying their occupational apprenticeship on the farm. In these situations women often battle for continued schooling for their sons, insisting on the importance of occupational options. This is also a clash about the importance of the continuity of the family enter-prise to which many farm women may have little commitment:

It is very important to the men that the boys take over. I can't understand this attachment to land, I can't see it. If this is what he wants [her son], but he is young and it is hard for them to know at sixteen what they want. His father is sixty four and feels he has to teach him now or he won't be around. I've promised him that we will get a welding machine so that he can develop other skills. (E5)

He [her son] has stayed at home here on the farm and I could have killed him that he didn't go on for something. He was very good at studying and they wanted him to go on in the school. . . I could kill H for wanting him to stay on the farm. (E20)

The difference between east and west is very important here because it highlights the bases of male power in family farming – patrimony and occupational apprenticeship – and how power and influence shift within the family as that power is undermined and full-time farming is no longer regarded as a desirable occupation. In the east where mothers see farming as being risky and stressful, they may wish their children to have other occupational options. But on the larger holdings this will be contested by fathers who can wield considerably more influence by virtue of their control over material resources which can provide a viable livelihood for a successor. As we have already seen in Chapter Five, one of the ways women deal with this is by distancing themselves from the farm operation.

Reproduction – Mothers and the Future of Family Farming

The analysis in this chapter has established farm women's influence on reproduction of the farm enterprise and on family farming as a social form, as well as on social reproduction, through their command over the education of farm children. It is in the sphere of education and socialisation of children, through the mother role, that farm women exert a critical influence on reproduction. The exceptional educational attainments of farm children can be understood as being due largely to farm mothers' recognition that education is the key to a secure occupation. Farm women are having a profound influence on the trajectory of family farming and on social forms in the wider society. It is in their role as mothers with primary responsibility for the successful settlement of their children, rather than as farm wives that they exercise the greatest influence on reproduction.

In the stem family system which has characterised Irish farming since the famine, a fundamental basis of male power was the ownership of the land and control over succession; male successors were apprenticed to their fathers who had a great deal of power over them (McCullagh, 1991). Reproducing the farm and the farm labour force was paramount, and the problem of how the remainder of the family were to be dispersed was effectively relegated to mothers. While fatherhood involved responsibility for farming apprenticeship, motherhood was constituted in terms of preparing children for an unknown world outside the family farm. Women embraced the challenge of preparing children for the wider society, not only because it gave them power and authority in a social form constructed on patriarchal lines, but also as a way of resisting patriarchal dominance and creating a separate sphere of influence.

This resistance itself has a gender dimension in that, in the case of daughters, it represents an attempt to ensure that the cycle of dependent farm wife is fractured and that the women of the next generation have better choices. In the case of sons it represents farm wives' disillusionment with farming as an occupation or, on smaller holdings, a recognition that to remain in farming will require pluriactivity. What is important is that it is in their role as mothers, who can influence children's achievements through their control over social reproduction, that this power is located. However powerless women might be in terms of control over property, labour, or capital, the constitution of Irish motherhood ensures their power over children. Motherhood as a source of power and influence has been somewhat neglected by sociologists who have focused mostly on the initial experiences of motherhood (Oakley, 1981; Boulton 1983). Scheper-Hughes (1979), analysing Irish rural families from a psychological perspective, did recognise the critical influence of the mother in mapping out a future for her children by deciding who should become teacher, civil servant or priest, and in raising daughters to be self-reliant and independent. Inglis (1987) argued that what he called the 'moral power' of mothers and their influence over their children's future was dependent on the authority of the Catholic Church until the 1960s, mothers being effectively 'moral agents' of the Catholic Church in the home. While Inglis sheds much light on how Irish motherhood was constituted in the nineteenth century, he underestimates the basis of the power of mothers, casting them as almost helpless dupes of the Catholic Church, even though he admits that falling fertility since the 1960s is evidence of the decline of Church influence. The crucial point is that even within the confines of patriarchal structures, women have always managed to fashion spheres of influence for themselves. This highlights the need, in the case of intra-family relations, to conceptualise negotiation and spheres of influence rather than purely coercion as critical dimensions of power.

In this chapter then we have uncovered farm women's strongest power base. By controlling the sphere of education and socialisation within the farm family, farm women are the chief architects of a pattern of remarkable educational participation among farm children. Their influence therefore extends well beyond the family farm to the constitution of Irish society and the social form of rural living. In earlier chapters we had discerned farm wives' impact on reproduction and associated it with resistance and negotiation, but here we can see that it is based, not just on contesting the patriarchal structures of family farming, but on the very way in which motherhood is constituted on Irish family farms. Women may not inherit the land but they do give birth to the new generation, and as mothers, they assume the primary responsibility for creating the conditions for a satisfactory life for their children. This responsibility, reinforced by economic realism and by dispassionate assessment of the prospects for family farming as a livelihood, is at the core of their influence on the three aspects of social reproduction outlined at the beginning of this chapter.

On smaller holdings, the expectation that successors will already have an off-farm job is leading to enterprise changes whereby moving to less labour intensive systems (from dairying) coincides with the ageing of parents and the realisation that farming in future will not be a full-time occupation. Nevertheless, family farming as a social form will survive as long as children can find jobs within reasonable distance from the farm, but also because of the enormous ideological commitment to farming, particularly on the part of fathers. Not surprisingly, farm mothers are less committed to farming except in cases where it may be seen as a desirable lifestyle. Their real interest is in securing the best possible occupational options for their children. Their remarkable success in this means that they play an important role in shaping not just the future of famil farming but the class structure of Irish society.

8

WOMEN IN FAMILY FARMING IN IRELAND

Conclusions and Reflections

Introduction

The starting point of this research was the phenomenon of women's invisibility in family farming and the associated prevalence of a unitary concept of the farm family which obscures the structured inequalities within it. The central concern of the analysis has been to de-construct the family farm and farm family in order to discern and articulate women's unique experience within them, and to discover farm women's influence on the reproduction of this social form and on the wider social formation. The research was therefore explicitly concerned with attempting to link micro social processes with the social order at the macro level. The investigation of women's involvement in production, consumption and reproduction on family farms has revealed the nature and extent of their influence. Irish farm women are considerably more powerful than has hitherto been acknowledged or documented, and this raises a number of theoretical and practical issues on which I would like to reflect in this final chapter.

These issues converge around a central point – put simply, it is that farm women are active agents in shaping the world around them. Therefore, ignoring their influence results in a very partial and distorted understanding of social processes, particularly the evolution of family farming. Recognition of women's influence in fact poses a major challenge to current theories of agricultural restructuring and the future of family farming in capitalist societies, including the quest for an approach which emphasises the importance of understanding social processes through the experiences of those involved. It also highlights the need for feminist theory and practice to accommodate women's resistance to patriarchal structures and the specificity of local conditions and cultures. The discovery that Irish farm women, within the context of a patriarchal structure of family farming, are actively shaping the future and pursuing their interests from their own unique perspective, in which personal experience and collective memory of subordination figure prominently, raises issues of broader significance for women's status, the reproduction of family farming and the evolution of Irish society generally. This chapter is organised around these themes which are all interrelated, so that the discussion also ranges across them as we draw out the implications of the analysis and link them to some of the issues raised in Chapter Two.

The Evolution of Family Farming

Recent debates in rural sociology concerning change and restructuring in European agriculture have been dominated by a commoditisation perspective which focuses on the relationship between family farming and the wider capitalist economy. The development of theory in this area has been influenced mainly by British and Dutch social scientists who have focused on family farming in some of the most capitalised parts of Europe (England, the Netherlands, Northern Italy). With the exception of the work of Whatmore (1991) in England, the work of commoditisation theorists while acknowledging the importance of intra-family processes in principle, have largely ignored them in empirical studies. When the plea to listen to what key participants say has been answered, it is still usually only male landholders who are spoken to. Subsequent theory building is based therefore on a gender-biased male view of the world, constructed around farming 'styles' or farmer 'logic' or 'farmers' expectation of the future.

In Irish rural sociology on the other hand, the political economy approach to understanding the evolution of agrarian structures has been much less prominent, perhaps because capitalist penetration into agriculture, at the level of the family farm (especially in terms of its internal relations) is less pronounced. There has been less focus on commoditisation and more on differentiation within the farming population and on the responses or 'survival strategies' of 'farmers'. Recent work on the survival strategies of farm families and on farmer logic has attributed the resilience of family farming on smallholdings to the remaining vestiges of a peasant system which has made smallholders in the west of Ireland particularly tenacious and resourceful. Little attention has been paid to the effects of the commoditisation process on the more commercialised farming sector – a minority of all family farms on which the majority of all production and income is generated. Questions concerning intra-family processes, such as whether women's actions affect continuity in family farming, and the significance of gender as a social division within farm families have received little theoretical or empirical scrutiny.

In this book I have sought to make a contribution to the debates about changing agrarian structures by attempting to demonstrate the significance of farm women's actions in shaping the evolution of family farming. As farm daughters, many farm women sought to avoid repli-cating the harsh lives of their mothers and fled rural Ireland in large numbers. Those who became farm wives and mothers have resisted patriarchy in ways which are having a profound affect on the evolution of Irish society both on and off the farm. The fact that women too are social actors with the capacity to shape and change the world around them can no longer be discounted or ignored. The assumption of the unitary farm family obscures not just women's subordination but also their responses to it.

The empirical investigation focused on women in the west and east of Ireland. The decision to select women from both of these regions was based not just on the observable differences between west and east in terms of the scale and commercialisation of farming, but also on the need to redress the regional imbalance in Irish rural sociology whereby much of the empirical research on agrarian restructuring has been car-ried out among smallholders in the west. Although a comparison between the two regions was not a primary objective of this research, it became inevitable at many points as the differences between them emerged from the responses of the farm women and their interpretations of their situations. These differences appear to be partly rooted in col-lective experiences which have some regional specificity, but they also appear to be associated with the size and degree of commercialisation of the farm enterprise, with commoditisation, with levels of income and material wealth, along with the contrasts in the local economies, includ-ing labour market opportunities.

Region then, has emerged in this study as a kind of proxy for a num-ber of factors, particularly farm size and commercialisation, which in turn appear to be associated with different 'cultures'. The value of the regional dimension has been to alert us to the different conditions which influence women's experience as farm wives and how they intersect in different ways. We have also been able to discern women's influence on farm continuity and how it varies in different farm situations, and to compare the trajectories of farming in the west and east, as well as farm wives' involvement in the construction of these different futures.

For instance farm wives' labour can be indispensable to the farm enterprise or their off-farm income may be crucial in insulating or rescuing the family from the risks associated with farming, thus enabling the family enterprise to continue and perhaps to expand further. Nevertheless, on many farms in the west there is little expectation that full-time farming will persist into the next generation. Farm wives there are actively engaged in ensuring that their children will have alternative occupational options. They expect that if their children do take up farming it will be on a part-time basis. In the east, on larger holdings, there is an expectation of succession to full-time farming, but here farm women are often somewhat disenchanted with farming as an occupation and seek to ensure that their children have other choices, often in contention with their husbands for whom farm continuity is a primary objective. What is indisputable is that women invariably have a distinct influence on continuity. This happens frequently through their direct involvement in the farm enterprise, but in any case occurs more profoundly through the family where, as mothers of potential successors, farm women are constructing the future for their children, a point to which we return below.

Women's Subordination and Empowerment – Marriage and Work

The challenge to theories of both agrarian change and the evolution of family farming which this research provides is only one side of the coin; the other is the issue of farm women's subordination and how it should be understood. From a feminist perspective family farming is clearly oppressive to women – their on-farm work is unpaid and publicly invisible, they do not usually inherit or own the land; and they are part of an industry which is publicly controlled by men and apparently bound by ideologies and cultural prescriptions which assign women to a subordinate status. Analysis of how this patriarchal regime extends to the micro-world of the farm family, and how women understand and deal with the constraints it imposes, raises some of the central issues of feminist theory. Among the most important of these are: whether the family is to be understood as the major site of women's exploitation; the influence of patriarchal ideology on women's lives; how power within the family is to be understood; and whether patriarchy and capitalism together reinforce women's subordination.

Within the family farm, the gendered organisation of work and capital have been perceived as the principal axis of patriarchal gender relations and the family itself as the locus of women's exploitation. The cumulative outcome of much of feminist theorising however, is a kind of patriarchal determinism which makes farm women appear powerless. The family may be the locus of women's oppression but this research has shown that it is within the family that we can also locate the major source of their influence. Although it has revealed clearly how patriarchal gender relations at the level of the family farm, together with ideology and culture, can constrain women it has also underlined the ways in which farm wives contest and negotiate patriarchal structures and the sources of their influence. In this context power is conceptualised as a process of negotiation, as 'power to', rather than the more absolutist 'power over'.

Examination of the circumstance of marriage of farm wives drew us immediately into the complexities of family life and some of the sources of women's subordination and empowerment. The willingness of those on smallholdings to marry into farming, when so many of their sisters were eschewing such an option, appeared to give some a kind of currency which enabled them to negotiate patriarchal structures. Nevertheless older women, especially in the west, recollect circumstances of marriage in which family obligations and the weight of ideology figure prominently. The constraints that they have felt in their own lives prompt them to endorse and help create new ideologies of privacy, sharing, and financial independence for their children which were unavailable to themselves. Younger women now live out these new images of family life by insisting on what they consider to be a 'modern marriage'. The importance of ideologies of both gender roles and family life in shaping the reality and meaning of women's lives is clear and not unexpected, given Hannan and Katsiaouni's (1977) earlier findings. Indeed this book began with an assertion of the significance of family and farm ideology in Ireland; the analysis has revealed the strength of ideological factors in setting the parameters of farm women's lives. What is particularly revealing however, is how women themselves respond to the constraints of ideology and culture by trying to change or circumvent them, if not for themselves, at least for their daughters. This finding again reinforces the need to see women as active agents in shaping the world around them.

Farm wives' engagement with farming from the beginning of their marriages was found to be almost unavoidable on smaller holdings, but on larger commercial farms, women often began their marriage by being more distant from the family farm, thus establishing a pattern of separation of home and business which is evident in work roles and consumption patterns as well. This suggests a possible link between the degree of commercialisation/commoditisation and women's involvement in the labour process – the critical question being whether commercialisation of the farm enterprise lessens women's influence and increases their subordination, or whether women seize the chance of avoiding engagement with farming to enhance their own autonomy and independence, and in the process relinquish any possible direct influence on the farm enterprise. These are issues which are central to some of the more recent debates in commoditisation theory about the link between family dynamics and commoditisation (Marsden et al., 1992). It may be that as commoditisation proceeds, women respond by disengaging from the family enterprise and creating their own sphere of influence in the home or in an off-farm occupation. The evidence from this research suggests that this happens only on the largest farms. However, while these women may be no longer involved directly in the farm labour process, they still exert a major influence on the evolution of family farming through their reproductive role in the farm family.

The majority of farm women in the study were actively engaged with the farm as a family enterprise and this emerged clearly when the labour process was examined. Avoiding dichotomous concepts often associated with the work of women in family businesses, such as productive/reproductive or use value/exchange value, the analysis focused on the totality of women's work for the family farm, paying particular attention to the working relationships. Farm wives' working relationships can reinforce their subordination or provide them with a means of lessening the constraints by which their day-to-day lives are circumscribed. The delineation of four categories of working relationships – farm helper, farm homemaker, working for the family farm, farm women in paid work – has helped to elucidate this.

The labour process on the farm is the principal site of male dominance in the case of those identified as *farm helpers*. They feel their subjugation keenly but feel powerless to change their assigned work roles which are bounded by their husbands' control over the farm and family and their own financial dependence. They 'fight back' by endeavouring to ensure that their daughters have better livelihood choices. A minority of farm women in the study were categorised as *farm homemakers* who remain in the domestic sphere and are relatively detached from the farm labour process. They are not, however, without influence since through their consumption and reproductive activities, particularly as mothers, they can have a significant affect on farm continuity. Their confinement to the domestic sphere, however, consigns them to the same limbo in which housewives everywhere find themselves – hidden, unrecorded, unpaid and dependent workers, without public status.

Farm wives who are *working for the family farm* on the other hand, have managed to negotiate a particular way of contesting patriarchal structures by evolving a working arrangement characterised more by partnership than male authority. Critical here is the nature of the conjugal contract and the relationships of affection and loyalty between spouses who are working jointly for what they consider worthwhile and valuable goals. These women recognise their own vocational competence and influence on a family enterprise which, despite the risks and uncertainties, offers much that they appreciate. Through their working relationships they have fashioned their own form of equality and are conscious of their strength and influence. The family farm is very much their own (even though they may not own the land) and their descriptions of their work for the farm are strongly associated with ideas of family solidarity and partnership with their husbands. That this has happened through negotiation of family relationships within an apparently patriarchal social form suggests that we need to bring family relationships much more to the fore when examining women's involvement in family enterprises. Patriarchal exploitation is clearly not the same for all women so that imposed labels such as that of 'head of household' may not 'fit' what is actually happening in the working relationship.

Among the most important sources of farm wives' empowerment which this research revealed was their involvement in non-farm work and their ownership of a personal income associated with it. Having a separate and distinct occupation and income, together with a (usually) higher level of educational attainment than her husband may not only strengthen a farm wife's bargaining position as she enters marriage with 'cultural capital', but may also shift the balance of power in marital negotiation over work roles. Women who have an off-farm job can achieve a different relationship to the family enterprise which arises from an acknowledgement of the significance of their earned income for its continuance. On smaller holdings, or those under financial pressure, their income is crucial for the continuance of the farming enterprise. Their contribution to the farm is therefore indirect, mediated by the market and highly dependent on local labour market conditions. The fact that it is so significant, however, strengthens the hand of these women in conjugal negotiation. In fact, these women are effectively using the competition between patriarchal family farming and capitalism for their own labour as a source of empowerment.

On larger, more commercialised farms, women's off-farm work allows them a separate vocational identity, and this often coincides with their own non-farm background and their remaining detached from day-to-day activities on the farm so that its significance as a family enterprise is less important to them. As a patriarchal enterprise, family farming can exist in parallel with their own vocational activities, as family capital which is owned and controlled by their husbands and in which their own direct labour involvement is minimal. They are nevertheless still tied to the family farm by their consumption and reproductive roles. Moreover, the fact that they are generating a separate income may release farm profits for reinvestment, a point to which we shall return below. The women in all categories of course remain primarily responsible for household work and child-rearing and, apart from those who have been able to use their off-farm work commitments to negotiate some sharing of household work, there is little evidence of significant male involvement, a predicament which is by no means unique to farm families.

Inside the Family – Dependency and Power

One of the distinctive features of this study is its focus on consumption and reproduction as well as on the labour process. The analysis of consumption revealed considerable inequalities in the distribution of resources inside the farm family. Not unexpectedly, the ownership of farms generally remains firmly and solely in the hands of husbands, particularly on the larger holdings in the east where the farm assets are extensive and valuable. In fact there are important differences between farm families in terms of the degree to which women manage and have access to family resources. On smaller holdings where income is scarce women were much more likely to be total money managers than on larger more commercial farms, where gender segregated arrangements, such as an allowance system, are more common. In some farm families, particularly those characterised by working relationships in which the farm wife could be said to be 'working for the family farm', all income is genuinely seen as family money. From the perspective of all farm wives, exclusion from farm ownership was a far less pressing source of constraint than day-to-day access to money or to other family resources such as the family car. Where control of such resources is strongly asymmetrical, women feel an acute sense of dependence and loss of personal autonomy which in some cases appears to be retrievable only in widowhood.

Women regard having their own incomes as the main route to avoiding such dependence; the generation and ownership of personal income through non-farm work was regarded by them as a way of securing independence and personal autonomy. Nevertheless, when they do engage in paid work, farm wives spend their money on the family rather than themselves. Women consistently say that they 'put themselves last' whether they have a personal income or not. In cases of income scarcity and poor returns from farming, the farm wife's income allows the family a higher standard of living than they might otherwise have been able to afford. The wife's income may enable the couple to acquire a mortgage, for instance. The significance of women's off-farm earnings as a source of empowerment was again evident here, as it was in the case of work discussed earlier.

However, women's acquisition and spending of their own incomes in this way has several other important implications for the evolution of family farming. We have mentioned already that women's incomes can insulate the farm family from the risks associated with farming (or indeed rescue the enterprise from financial difficulties) and so provide a higher standard of living. By the same token, diversion of women's earnings to current domestic and family expenditure on larger commercial holdings can allow male farmers to engage in accumulation strategies which can ultimately strengthen patriarchal control, since most farm women do not have any ownership rights to the land and capital. Moreover, separation of 'farm' and 'family' income in this way appears to reinforce the detachment of farm and household, thus changing the character of 'family farming'. Contemporary farm wives may well be the last generation of women so actively engaged with the farm enterprise.

Is this then, the shape of things to come? Will farm wives in the future be less involved in the family enterprise and will this alter the nature of family farming? Few farm women, regardless of their own involvement in the family enterprise, foresee a future for their daughters in family farming. Those who feel strongly constrained by patriarchal family relations in the labour process and within the farm family, try to construct a future for their daughters in which the cycles of dependent wives will be fractured and they as the next generation will have better choices. Even those who are 'working for the family farm' and have a strong sense of their own autonomy do not see their daughters replicating their roles in the next generation. Indeed like all farm mothers they too are actively shaping a future in which their daughters 'cultural capital' is maximised. In the event of their daughters marrying into farming, mothers seek to ensure that they will have the opportunity to have their own career and personal income, and daughters themselves concur with this.

This brings us to the most important source of farm women's power which this research has uncovered through its focus on reproduction – their influence on the future through their role as mothers. It is in their role as mothers that Irish farm women exert the greatest influence on the future of family farming. Ironically, the very patriarchal structures which constrain them can also be seen as sources of their empowerment by constituting them in the category of wife/mother and assigning to them the crucial tasks of child-rearing, socialisation and education culminating in the placement of the next generation. Regardless of whether farm women can realise their personal interests, they have for many decades used their influence as mothers to secure for their children livelihood options outside of family farming. Their commitment to success in this is reflected in the remarkable levels of educational participation among farm children.

Farm women's control over children's education and associated occupational achievements has had an enormous impact not just on family farming itself but on the class structure of Irish society. Women's commitment to securing the future for their children is associated with their resistance to the patriarchal structures of family farming and is reinforced by their perception of the need for farm children to have other career options besides farming. Women's influence in this sphere has been missed by much of the empirical research on farm women which focuses on the present generation,[1] and by the theoretical work which largely ignores their role in social reproduction.

It might also be suggested that feminist theory needs to pay more attention to issues of power and influence within the family, and find ways of theorising women's influence as well as their subordination. Theoretically and empirically, women's subordination within the family has now been well established by feminists. However some feminist theorising of women's subordination has led to a kind of theoretical cul de sac whereby patriarchal structures become determinate and the ways in which women negotiate and resist them cannot easily be accommodated. This research has suggested that a shift in focus to women as active agents who challenge and negotiate patriarchal structures or even use the tension between capitalism and patriarchy for their own ends, presents an exciting agenda for future feminist theorising, without compromising its fundamental principles.

Such theorising would be likely to reveal women to themselves in a way that is easily recognisable. Much feminist theorising does not resonate entirely with contemporary women who, while aware of the structures which constrain them, are also conscious of the enormous complexity of intra-family relationships and the diversity of ways in

---

1. A notable exception is Gasson's (1987) study of farmers' daughters in the south of England. She found that only 13 percent of farmers' daughters married farmers and that their home farms were larger than average with a mean size of 195 hectares.

which these relationships are negotiated in practice. Put simply, feminist theories concerning women in families or in family businesses need to be redirected away from the determinism associated with theories of exploitation, in order to acknowledge women's room to manoeuvre, and present them as consciously engaged in shaping and influencing the world around them. Indeed, it appears that family businesses such as farming can offer unique opportunities for the construction of pragmatically balanced working and affectional relationships between women and men, in which traditional role boundaries shift imperceptibly over time through negotiations which are directed towards collective rather than individual goals. This suggests that we need to modify the idea of the family as universally exploitative and acknowledge that the labour process in some circumstances can actually provide a way of constructing egalitarian gender relationships. Women who work for the family farm expressed considerable satisfaction with their lot, while at the same time freely acknowledging the constraints of a wider gender order by which all women are subordinated, and the difficulties and drawbacks of trying to make a living from farming. Indeed the dualism associated with the well-worn dichotomies of the separation of public and private spheres, exchange values and use values, women's double burden or divided lives, seem unhelpful (and irrelevant?) for comprehending the situation of these women. But they may well be the last generation of farm women who take on the occupation of farming in this way (apart from those who select it as a 'lifestyle' option), as future farm wives are likely to want to work off the farm after marriage. Whether such relationships are being negotiated and achieved in non-farm family contexts and their meaning to the individuals involved, are important issues for future investigation.

Most importantly of all, feminist theory needs to pay a great deal more attention to what it has heretofore largely neglected and what this study has shown to be at the core of women's influence – their power as mothers. In this, the emphasis should be not just on motherhood as a socially constructed role but on mothers as critical actors in the process of social reproduction. This study, in focusing on the micro level of the farm family, has shown how farm women as mothers have a continuing and significant influence on the future of family farming and on the macro structures of Irish society. It is unlikely that such influence is unique to farm women. More attention to women's reproductive role in its widest sense should reveal the reality of their unacknowledged and largely unexplored influence on the evolution of Irish society.

BIBLIOGRAPHY

ACOT (Council for Development in Agriculture), (1981) *Report of the ACOT Expert Group on Agricultural Education and Training*, Dublin: ACOT.

Almas, R. and Haugen, M.S. (1988) 'Norwegian gender roles in transition: the masculinization hypothesis in the past and in the future', Rural Research Paper No. 1, University of Trondheim Rural Research Group.

Alston, M. (1995) 'Women and their work on Australian farms', *Rural Sociology*, 60(3), 521–32.

Amin, S. and Vergopolous, K. (1974) *La Question Paysanne et le Capitalisme*, Paris: Anthropos.

Arensberg, C.M. and Kimball, S.T. (1968) *Family and Community in Ireland*, Harvard: Harvard University Press (first edition 1940, re-issued in 1968).

Arkleton Trust (1992) 'Farm household adjustment in western Europe, 1987–1991', Vols I and II, Inverness: Arkleton Trust Research.

Banaji, J. (1980) 'A summary of selected parts of Kautsky's The Agrarian Question' reprinted in Buttel, F. and Newby, H. (eds) *The Rural Sociology of the Advanced Societies*, London: Croom Helm.

Barrett, M. (1980) *Women's Oppression Today: Problems in Marxist Feminist Analysis*, London: Verso.

Barrett, M. and McIntosh, M. (1982) *The Anti-Social Family*, London: Verso.

Bauwens, A. and Loeffen, T. (1983) 'The changing economic and social position of the farmer's wife in The Netherlands', Paper to 12th European Congress for Rural Sociology, Budapest.

Beal, J. (1986) *Women in Ireland: Voices of Change*, London: Macmillan.

Bell, C., Bryden, J.M., Fuller, A.M, MacKinnon, N. and Spearman, M. (1990) 'Economic and social change in Europe, participation by farm women in the labour market and implications for change', in European Commission Childcare Network, *Childcare Needs of Rural Families*, Seminar Report, Brussels: Commission of the European Communities.

Bennholdt-Thomsen, V. (1981) 'Subsistence production and extended reproduction', in Young, K., Wolkowitz, C. and McCullagh, R. (eds) *Of Marriage and the Market: Women's Subordination in International Perspective*, London: CSE Books.

Bensten, M. (1969) 'The political economy of women's liberation', *Monthly Review*, 21(4).

Berlan Darque, M. (1988) 'The division of labour and decision-making in farming couples: power and negotiation', *Sociologia Ruralis*, 28(4), 271–92.

Bernstein, H. (1977) 'Notes on capital and peasantry', *Journal of African Political Economy*, 10, 60–73.

Bernstein, H. (1986) 'Is there a concept of petty commodity production generic to capitalism?', Paper to European Congress for Rural Sociology, Portugal.

Blanc, M. and MacKinnon, N. (1990) 'Gender relations and the family farm in Western Europe', *Journal of Rural Studies*, 6(4), 401–5.

Boserup, E. (1970) *Women's Role in Economic Development*, London: George Allen and Unwin.

Boulding, E. (1980) 'The labour of US farm women: a knowledge gap', *Sociology of Work and Occupations*, 7(3), 261–90.

Boulton, M.G. (1983) *On Being a Mother*, London: Tavistock.

Bouquet, M. (1982) 'Production and reproduction of family farms in south-west England', *Sociologia Ruralis*, 22(3–4), 227–41.

Bouquet, M. (1984) 'Women's work in rural south west England', in Long, N. (ed.) *Family and Work in Rural Societies*, London: Tavistock.

Bourdieu, P. (1972) 'Marriage strategies as strategies of social reproduction', in Forster, R. and Ranum, O. (eds) *Family and Society: Selections from the Annales*, Baltimore: John Hopkins University Press.

Bourdieu, P. (1977) *Outline of a Theory of Practice*, Cambridge: Cambridge University Press.

Bourke, J. (1991) 'Women, economics and power: Irish women 1880–1914', *Irish Home Economics Journal*, 1(2), 3–16.

Braithwaite, M. (1994) *The Economic Role and Situation of Women in Rural Areas*, European Commission, Special Issue of *Green Europe*, Brussels.

Brannen, J. (1992) 'Combining qualitative and quantitative approaches: an overview', in Brannen, J. (ed.) *Mixing Methods: Qualitative and Quantitative Research*, Aldershot: Avebury.

Brannen, J. and Wilson, G. (eds) (1987) *Give and Take in Families*, London: Allen and Unwin.

Breen, R. (1983) 'Farm servanthood in Ireland, 1900–1940', *Economic History Review*, 36(1), 87–102.

Breen, R. (1984) *Education and the Labour Market: Work and Unemployment among Recent Cohorts of Irish School Leavers*, Dublin: Economic and Social Research Institute.

Breen, R., Hannan, D., Rottman, D., and Whelan, C. (1990) *Understanding Contemporary Ireland: State, Class and Development in the Republic of Ireland*, Dublin: Gill and Macmillan.

Brody, H. (1973) *Inishkillane: Change and Decline in the West of Ireland*, London: Allen Lane.

Brown, C. (1981) 'Mothers, fathers and children: from private to public patriarchy', in Sargent, L. (ed.) *Women and Revolution: The Unhappy Marriage of Marxism and Feminism*, London: Pluto Press.

Bryman, A. (1988) *Quality and Quantity in Social Research*, London: Unwin Hyman.

Bryman, A. (1992) 'Quantitative and qualitative research: further reflections on their integration', in Brannen, J. (ed.) *Mixing Methods: Qualitative and Quantitative Research*, Aldershot: Avebury.

Buchanan, W.I., Errington, A.J. and Giles, A.K. (1982) 'The farmer's wife: her role in the management of the business', Study No. 2, Farm Management Unit, University of Reading.

Bunreacht na hÉireann (Constitution of Ireland) (1937) Dublin: Government Publications.

Burgoyne, C. (1990) 'Money in marriage: how patterns of allocation both reflect and conceal power', *Sociological Review*, 38(4), 635–65.

Buttel, F. (1982) 'The political economy of agriculture in advanced industrial societies: some observations on theory and method', *Current Perspectives in Social Theory*, 3, 27–55.

Central Statistics Office (1994a) *Census of Population 1991*, Government Publications, Dublin: Stationary Office.

Central Statistics Office (1994b) *Census of Agriculture 1991*, Government Publications, Dublin: Stationary Office.

Charles, N. and Kerr, M. (1987) 'Just the way it is: gender and age differences in family food consumption', in Brannen, J. and Wilson, G. (eds) *Give and Take in Families*, London: Allen and Unwin.

Chayanov, A.V. (1966) in Thorner, D., Smith, R. and Kerblay, B. (eds) *The Theory of Peasant Economy*, (first edition 1925) London: Irwin.

Cheal, D. (1991) *Family and the State of Theory*, London: Harvester Wheatsheaf.

Cicourel, A.V. 1981 'Notes on the integration of micro and macro levels of analysis', in Knorr-Cetina K. and Cicourel, A.V. (eds) *Advances in Social Theory and Methodology*, London: Routledge and Kegan Paul.

Clancy, P. (1988) *Who Goes to College*, Dublin: Higher Education Authority.

Clancy, P. (1995) *Access to College: Patterns of Continuity and Change*, Dublin: Higher Education Authority.

Close, P. (1985) 'Family form and economic production', in Close, P. and Collins, R. (eds) *Family and Economy in Modern Society*, London: Macmillan.

Coleman, G. and Elbert, S. (1984) 'Farming families: the farm needs everyone', in Schwarzweller, H. K. (ed.) *Research in Rural Sociology and Development: Focus on Agriculture, Vol. I*, Greenwich: JAI Press.

Collins, R. (1981) 'Micro-translation as a theory-building strategy', in Knorr-Cetina K. and Cicourel, A.V. (eds) *Advances in Social Theory and Methodology*, London: Routledge and Kegan Paul.

Collins, R. (1985) 'Horses for courses: ideology and the division of domestic labour', in Close, P. and Collins, R. (eds) *Family and Economy in Modern Society*, London: Macmillan.

Commins, P., Cox, P., Curry, J. (1978) *Rural Areas: Change and Development*, Dublin: National Economic and Social Council.

Commins, P. and Keane, M. (1994) *Developing the Rural Economy: Problems, Programmes and Prospects*, Dublin: National Economic and Social Council.

Commission on Emigration and Other Population Problems 1948–1954, (1954) *Reports*, Dublin: The Stationary Office.

Connell, R.W. (1987) *Gender and Power*, Cambridge: Polity Press.

Conway, A.G. (1976) 'Farm performance and structure – alternative paths for adjustment', in *Agricultural Development: Prospects and Possibilities*, Dublin: An Foras Taluntais.

Conway, A.G. and O'Hara, P. (1984) *Irish Case Study to Identify Strategies for Integrated Rural Development*, Vols I–IV, Report to the European Commission, Brussels.

Conway, A.G. and O'Hara, P. (1986) 'Education of farm children', *The Economic and Social Review*, 17(4), 253–76.

Cowan, R.S. (1983) *More Work for Mother: The Ironies of Household Technology from Open Hearth to the Microwave*, New York: Basic Books.

Crow, G. (1989) 'The use and concept of "strategy" in recent sociological literature', *Sociology*, 23(1), 1–24.

Curtin, C. (1986) 'The peasant family farm and commoditisation in the West of Ireland', in Long, N., Ploeg, J.D. van der, Curtin, C. and Box, L. (eds) *The Commoditisation Debate: Labour Process, Strategy and Social Network*, Wageningen: Agricultural University, Papers of the Department of Sociology, 17.

Curtin, C. and Varley, T. (1987) 'Marginal men? Bachelor farmers in a West of Ireland community', in Curtin, C., Jackson, P. and O'Connor, B. (eds) *Gender in Irish Society*, Galway: Galway University Press.

Dalla Costa, M. (1972) *Women and the Subversion of the Community*, Bristol: Falling Wall Press.

Davis, J. (1980) 'Capitalist agricultural development and the exploitation of the propertied labourer', in Buttel, F. and Newby, H. (eds) *The Rural Sociology of Advanced Societies*, London: Croom Helm.

Delphy, C. (1984) *Close to Home*, London: Hutchinson.

Delphy, C. and Leonard, D. (1992) *Familiar Exploitation: A New Analysis of Marriage in Contemporary Societies*, Cambridge: Polity Press.

Department of Agriculture (1990) *Agriculture and Food Policy Review*, Dublin: Department of Agriculture.

Devault, M. (1990) 'Talking and listening from women's standpoint: Feminist strategies for interviewing and analysis', *Social Problems*, 37(1), 96–116.

Duggan, C. (1987) 'Farming women or farmers' wives? Women in the farming press', in Curtin, C., Jackson P. and O'Connor, B. (eds) *Gender in Irish Society*, Galway: Galway University Press.

Edgell, S. (1980) *Middle-Class Couples*, London: Allen and Unwin.

Edholm, F., Harris, O. and Young, K. (1977) 'Conceptualising women', *Critique of Anthropology*, 3 (9/10), 101–30.

Eichler, M. (1980) *The Double Standard*, London: Croom Helm.

Eisenstein, H. (1985) *Contemporary Feminist Thought*, London: Unwin.

Elbert, S. (1988) 'Women and farming: changing structures, changing roles', in Haney, W.G. and Knowles, J.B. (eds) *Women and Farming: Changing Roles, Changing Structures*, Boulder: Westview Press.

Engels, F. (1942) *The Origin of the Family, Private Property and the State*, New York: International Publishers.

European Parliament Directorate General for Research (1994) *Situation, Status and Prospects of Women in Agriculture*, Luxembourg: European Parliament Working Paper.

Fahey, T. (1990) 'Measuring the female labour supply: conceptual and procedural problems in Irish official statistics', *Economic and Social Review*, 21(2), 163–91.

Fassinger, M. and Schwarzweller, H.K. (1984) 'The work of farm women', in Schwarzweller, H.K. (ed.) *Research in Rural Sociology and Development: Focus on Agriculture*, Vol.I, Greenwich: JAI Press.

Fielding, N.G. (ed.) (1988) *Actions and Structure: Research Methods and Social Theory*, London: Sage.

Finch, J. (1983) *Married to the Job: Wives' Incorporation in Men's Work*, London: Allen and Unwin.

Finch, J. (1984) 'It's great to have someone to talk to: the ethics and politics of interviewing women', in Bell, C. and Roberts, H. (eds) *Social Researching: Politics, Problems, Practice*, London: Routledge and Kegan Paul.

Finch, J. (1989) *Family Obligations and Social Change*, Cambridge: Polity Press.

Firestone, S. (1970) *The Dialectic of Sex*, London: Jonathan Cape.

Fitzpatrick, D. (1986) '"A share of the honeycomb": education, emigration and Irishwomen', *Continuity and Change*, 1(2), 217–34.

Fox, B. (1980) 'Women's double work day: twentieth century changes in the reproduction of daily life', in Fox, B. (ed.) *Hidden in the Household*, Ontario: the Women's Press.

Friedmann, H. (1978) 'World market, state and family farm: social bases of household production in the era of wage labour', *Comparative Studies in Society and History*, 20(4), 545–86.

Friedmann, H. (1980) 'Household production and the national economy: concepts for the analysis of agrarian formations', *The Journal of Peasant Studies*, 7(2), 158–84.

Friedmann, H. (1981) 'The family farm in advanced capitalism: outline of a theory of simple commodity production in agriculture', Paper to American Sociological Association, Toronto.

Friedmann, H. (1986a) 'Patriarchy and property; a reply to Goodman and Redclift', *Sociologia Ruralis*, 26(2), 186–93.

Friedmann, H. (1986b) 'Family enterprises in agriculture: structural limits and political possibilities', in Cox, G., Lowe, P. and Winter, M. (eds) *Agriculture: People and Policies*, London: Allen and Unwin.

Garcia-Ramon, M.D. and Canoves, G. (1988) 'The role of women in the family farm: the case of Catalonia', *Sociologia Ruralis*, 28(4), 271–92.

Gardiner, J. (1976) 'Political economy of domestic labour in capitalist society', in Barker Leonard, D. and Allen, S. (eds) *Dependence and Exploitation in Work and Marriage*, London: Longman.

Gasson, R. (1980a) 'The farm woman's work is never done', *Farmer's Weekly*, 92(9), 89–95.

Gasson, R. (1980b) 'Roles of farm women in England', *Sociologia Ruralis*, 20(3), 165–80.

Gasson, R. (1987) 'Careers of farmers' daughters', *Farm Management*, 6(7), 309–17.

Gasson, R. (1989) *Farm Work by Farmers' Wives*, Farm Business Unit, Occasional Paper No. 15, Ashford: Wye College.

Gasson, R. (1992) 'Farm wives – their contribution to the farm business', *Journal of Agricultural Economics*, 43(1), 74–87.

Gasson, R. and Winter, M. (1992) 'Gender relations and farm household pluriactivity', *Journal of Rural Studies*, 8, 573–84.

Geisler, C.C., Waters, M.F. and Eadie, K.L. (1985) 'The changing structure of female land ownership 1946–1978', *Rural Sociology*, 50(1), 74–87.

Gelsthorpe, L. (1992) 'Response to Martyn Hammersley's paper "On feminist methodology"', *Sociology*, 26(2), 213–18.

Gershuny, J. (1983) *Social Innovation and the Division of Labour*, Oxford: Oxford University Press.

Gibbon, P. (1973) 'Arensberg and Kimball revisited', *Economy and Society*, 2(4), 479–98.

Giddens, A. (1976) *New Rules of Sociologica Method*, London: Hutchinson.

Giddens, A. (1979) *Central Problems in Social Theory*, London: Macmillan.

Goodman, D. and Redclift, M. (1985) 'Capitalism, petty commodity production and the farm enterprise', *Sociologia Ruralis*, 25(3/4), 231–47.

Goodman, D. and Redclift, M. (1988) 'Problems in analysing the agrarian transition in Europe', *Comparative Studies in Society and History*, 30(4), 784–91.

Goody, J. (1976) *Production and Reproduction*, Cambridge: Cambridge University Press.

Guinnane, T.W. (1992) 'Age at leaving home in rural Ireland 1901–1911', *Journal of Economic History*, 52(3), 651–74.

Hammersley, M. (1992a) 'Deconstructing the qualitative-quantitative divide', in Brannen, J. (ed.) *Mixing Methods: Qualitative and Quantitative Research*, Aldershot: Avebury.

Hammersley, M. (1992b) 'On Feminist methodology', *Sociology*, 26(2), 187–206.

Hannan, D.F. (1970) *Rural Exodus: A Study of the Forces Influencing the Large-Scale Migration of Irish Rural Youth*, London and Dublin: Geoffry Chapman.

Hannan. D.F. (1972) 'Kinship, neighbourhood and social change in Irish rural communities', *Economic and Social Review*, 3(2), 163–88.

Hannan, D.F. (1979) *Displacement and Development: Class, Kinship and Social Change in Irish Rural Communities*, Dublin: Economic and Social Research Institute.

Hannan, D.F. (1982) 'Peasant models and the understanding of social and cultural change in rural Ireland', in Drudy, P.J. (ed.) *Ireland: Land, Politics and People*, Cambridge: Cambridge University Press.

Hannan, D.F. and Commins, P. (1992) 'The significance of small-scale landholders in Ireland's socio-economic transformation', in Goldthorpe, J. (ed.) *The Development of Industrial Society in Ireland*, Oxford: Oxford University Press.

Hannan, D.F. and Commins, P. (1993) *Factors Affecting Land Availability for Afforestation*, Dublin: Economic and Social Research Institute.

Hannan, D.F. and Katsiaouni, L. (1977) *Traditional Families? From Culturally Prescribed to Negotiated Roles in Farm Families*, Dublin: Economic and Social Research Institute.

Hannan, D.F. and O'Riain, S. (1993) *Pathways to Adulthood in Ireland: Causes and Consequences of Success and Failure in Transitions Among Irish Youth*, Dublin: Economic and Social Research Institute.

Harding, S. (ed.) (1987) *Feminism and Methodology*, Bloomington: Indiana University Press.

Harrison, J. (1974) 'The political economy of housework', *Bulletin of the Conference of Socialist Economists*, 3, 35–52.

Hartmann, H.I. (1979) 'The unhappy marriage of Marxism and Feminism: towards a more progressive union', *Capital and Class*, 8, 1–33.

Higgins, J. (1983) *A Study of Part-time Farmers in the Republic of Ireland*, Dublin: An Foras Taluntais.

Higher Education Authority (1995) *Interim Report of the Steering Committee's Technical Working Group*, Dublin: HEA.

Hill, F. (1980) 'Farm women: a challenge to scholarship', *The Rural Sociologist*, 1(6), 376–82.

Inglis, T. (1987) *Moral Monopoly: The Catholic Church in Modern Irish Society*, Dublin: Gill and Macmillan.

Janvry, A.de (1980) 'Social differentiation in agriculture and the ideology of neopopulism', in Buttel, F. and Newby, H. (eds) *The Rural Sociology of the Advanced Societies*, London: Croom Helm.

Johnson, R. and Conway, A.G. (1976) 'Factors associated with growth in farm output', Paper to Agricultural Economics Society of Ireland, Dublin.

Jones, C. and Rosenfeld, R. (1981) *American Farm Women: Findings from a National Survey*, NORC Report No. 130, Chicago: National Opinion Research Centre.

Keating, N.C. and Little, H.M. (1994) 'Getting into it: Farm roles and careers of New Zealand women', *Rural Sociology*, 59(3), 720–36.

Kelleher, C. and O'Hara, P. (1978) *Adjustment Problems of Low-Income Farmers*, Dublin: An Foras Taluntais.

Kelleher, C. and O'Mahony, A. (1984) *Marginalisation in Irish Agriculture*, Dublin: An Foras Taluntais.

Kennedy, R. (1973) *The Irish: Emigration, Marriage and Fertility*, Berkeley: University of California Press.

Knorr-Cetina K. and Cicourel, A. V. (1981) *Advances in Social Theory and Methodology*, London: Routledge and Kegan Paul.

Knorr-Cetina, K. (1981) 'The micro-sociological challenge of macro-sociology', in Knorr-Cetina K. and Cicourel, A.V. (eds) *Advances in Social Theory and Methodology*, London: Routledge and Kegan Paul.

Knorr-Cetina, K. (1988) 'The micro-social order', in Fielding, N.G. (ed.) *Actions and Structure: Research Methods and Social Theory*, London: Sage.

Land, H. (1977) 'Inequalities in large families: more of the same or different?' in Chester, R. and Peel, J. (eds) *Equalities and Inequalities in Family Life*, London: Academic Press.

Layder, D. (1993) *New Strategies in Social Research*, Cambridge: Polity Press.

Lee, J. (1989) *Ireland, 1912–1985*, Cambridge: Cambridge University Press.

Leeuwis, C. (1987) 'Marginalisation misunderstood', Research Report, Wageningen: Agricultural University, Rural Sociology.

Lenin, V.I. (1946) *Capitalism and Agriculture*, New York: International Publishers.

Lentin, R. (1993) 'Feminist research methodologies: A separate paradigm? Notes for a debate', *Irish Journal of Sociology*, 3, 119–38.

Leonard, D. (1980) *Sex and Generation: A Study of Courtship and Weddings*, London: Tavistock.

Long, N. (ed.) (1984) *Family and Work in Rural Societies*, London: Tavistock.

Long, N. (1986) 'Commoditization: thesis and antithesis', in Long, N., Ploeg, J.D. van der, Curtin, C. and Box, L. *The Commoditisation Debate: Labour Process, Strategy and Social Network*, Papers of the Department of Sociology, 17, Wageningen: Agricultural University.

Long, N. (1990) 'From paradigm lost to paradigm regained? The case for an actor-oriented sociology of development', *European Review of Latin American and Caribbean Studies*, 49.

Long, N. (1992) 'Introduction', in Long, N. and Long, A. (eds) *Battlefields of Knowledge*, London: Routledge.

Long, N., Ploeg, J.D. van der, Curtin, C. and Box, L. (1986) *The Commoditization Debate: Labour Process, Strategy and Social Network*, Papers of the Department of Sociology, 17, Wageningen: Agricultural University.

McCullagh, C. (1991) 'A tie that blinds: family and ideology in Ireland', *The Economic and Social Review*, 22(3), 199–211.

McDonough, R. and Harrison, R. (1978) 'Patriarchy and relations of production', in Kuhn, A. and Wolpe, A. (eds) *Feminism and Materialism*, London: Routledge and Kegan Paul.

McNabb, P. (1964) 'Demography' and 'Social Structure' in Newman. J. (ed.) *The Limerick Rural Survey 1958–1964*, Tipperary: Muintir na Tire.

Mackintosh, M. (1977) 'Reproduction and patriarchy: a critique of Claude Meillassoux, *Femmes, Greniers et Capitaux*', *Capital and Class*, 2, 119–27.

Mackintosh, M. (1981) 'Gender and economics: the sexual division of labour and the subordination of women', in Young, K., Wolkowitz, C. and McCullagh, R. (eds) *Of Marriage and the Market: Women's Subordination in International Perspective*, London: CSE Books.

Mahon, E. (1994) 'Feminist research: A reply to Lentin', *Irish Journal of Sociology*, 4, 165–69.

Mann, S.A. (1990) *Agrarian Capitalism in Theory and Practice*, Chapel Hill, North Carolina: University of North Carolina Press.

Mann, S.A. and Dickinson, J.M. (1978) 'Obstacles to the development of a capitalist agriculture', *Journal of Peasant Studies*, 5, 466–81.

Marsden, T. (1991) 'Theoretical issues in the continuity of petty commodity production', in Whatmore, S., Lowe, P. and Marsden, T. (eds) *Rural Enterprise: Shifting Perspectives on Small-Scale Production*, London: David Fulton.

Marsden, T.K., Munton, R.J., Whatmore, S.J. and Little, J.K. (1986a) 'Towards a political economy of capitalist agriculture: a British perspective', *International Journal of Urban and Regional Research*, 10, 498–521.

Marsden, T.K., Munton, R.J., Whatmore, S.J. and Little, J.K. (1986b) 'The restructuring process: economic centrality in capitalist agriculture', *Journal of Rural Studies*, 2(4), 271–80.

Marsden, T.K., Munton, R.J. and Ward, N. (1992) 'Incorporating social trajectories into uneven agrarian development: farm businesses in upland and lowland Britain', *Sociologia Ruralis*, 32(4), 408–30.

Marx Ferree, M. (1990) 'Beyond separate spheres: feminism and family research', *Journal of Marriage and the Family*, 52, 866–84.

Marx, K. (1976) *Capital*, Vols I and III, Harmondsworth: Penguin.

Meillassoux, C. (1981) *Maidens, Meals and Money*, Cambridge: Cambridge University Press.

Messenger, J. (1969) *Inis Beag - Isle of Ireland*, New York: Holt, Rinehart and Winston.

Mies, M. (1983) 'Towards a methodology for feminist research', in Bowles, G. and Duelli-Klein, R. (eds) *Theories of Women's Studies*, London: Routledge and Kegan Paul.

Mitchell, J. (1971) *Women's Estate*, Harmondsworth: Penguin.

Moore, H. L. (1988) *Feminism and Anthropology*, Cambridge: Polity Press.

Morris, L. (1990) *The Workings of the Household*, Cambridge: Polity Press.

Morris, L. (1993) 'Household finance management and the labour market: a case study in Hartlepool', *Sociological Review*, 41(3), 507–35.

Moser, P. (1993) 'Rural economy and female emigration in the West of Ireland 1936–1956', in Byrne, P., Conroy, J. and Hayes, A. (eds) *U.C.G. Women's Studies Centre Review*, 3, 41–51.

Mottura, G. and Pugliese, E. (1980) 'Capitalism in agriculture and capitalistic agriculture: the Italian case', in Buttel F. and Newby H. (eds) *The Rural Sociology of the Advanced Societies*, London: Croom Helm.

Oakley, A. (1974) *The Sociology of Housework*, Oxford: Martin Robertson.

Oakley, A. (1980) *Women Confined: Towards a Sociology of Childbirth*, Oxford: Martin Robertson.

Oakley, A. (1981) 'Interviewing women: a contradiction in terms', in Roberts, H. (ed.) *Doing Feminist Research*, London: Routledge and Kegan Paul.

Oakley, A. (1992) *Social Support and Motherhood: The Natural History of a Research Project*, Oxford: Basil Blackwell.

O'Connor, P. (1990) 'The adult mother-daughter relationship: a uniquely and universally close relationship?' *Sociological Review*, 38(2), 293–23.

O'Connor, P. (1992) *Friendships Between Women: A Critical Review*, London: Harvester Wheatsheaf.

O'Hara, P. (1985) 'A development perspective for the West of Ireland: Some recent research and its implications', in Conway, A.G. and O'Hara, P. (eds) *Living and Working in the West: Prospects and Challenges for the Future*, Dublin: An Foras Taluntais.

O'Hara, P. (1986) 'CAP socio-structural policy: a new approach to an old problem?' in *The Changing CAP and its Implications*, Dublin: An Foras Taluntais.

O'Hara, P. (1987a) 'Farm women: concerns and values of an undervalued workforce', UCD Women's Studies Forum, Working Paper No. 2, Dublin: University College Dublin.

O'Hara, P. (1987b) 'What became of them? West of Ireland women in the labour force', in Curtin, C., Jackson P. and O'Connor, B. (eds) *Gender in Irish Society*, Galway: Galway University Press.

O'Hara, P. (1990) 'Prospects for farm women' in *Women and the Completion of the Internal Market*, Dublin: Department of Labour.

Pahl, J. (1989) *Money and Marriage*, London: Macmillan.

Pahl, J. (1991) 'Money and power in marriage', in Abbott, P. and Wallace, C. (eds) *Gender, Power and Sexuality*, London: Macmillan.

Pahl, R. (1984) *Divisions of Labour*, Oxford: Blackwell.

Pfeffer, M.J. (1989) 'The feminization of production on part-time farms in the Federal Republic of Germany', *Rural Sociology*, 54(1), 60–73.

Pile, S. (1991) 'Securing the future: "survival strategies" amongst Somerset dairy farmers', *Sociology*, 25(2), 255–74.

Ploeg, J.D. van der (1986) 'The agricultural labour process and commoditisation', in Long, N., Ploeg, J.D. van der., Curtin, C. and Box, L. *The Commoditisation Debate: Labour Process, Strategy and Social Network*, Papers of the Department of Sociology, 17, Wageningen: Agricultural University.

Ploeg, J.D. van der (1990) *Labour, Markets and Agricultural Production*, Boulder: Westview Press.

Ploeg, J.D. van der (1993) 'Rural sociology and the new agrarian question: a perspective from The Netherlands', *Sociologia Ruralis*, 33(2), 240–60.

Power, R. and Roche, M. (1991) *National Farm Survey 1990*, Dublin: Teagasc.

Power, R. and Roche, M. (1995) *National Farm Survey 1994*, Dublin: Teagasc.

Ramazanoglu, C. (1992) 'On feminist methodology: male reason versus female empowerment', *Sociology*, 26(2), 207–12.

Redclift, M. (1986) 'Survival strategies in rural Europe: continuity and change', *Sociologia Ruralis*, 26(3/4), 218–27.

Redclift, N. (1985) 'The contested domain: gender, accumulation and the labour process', in Redclift, N. and Mignione, E. (eds) *Beyond Employment: Household, Gender and Subsistence*, London: Basil Blackwell.

Redclift, N. and Mignione, E. (eds) (1985) *Beyond Employment: Household, Gender and Subsistence*, London: Basil Blackwell.

Redclift, N. and Whatmore, S. (1990) 'Household, consumption and livelihood: ideologies and issues in rural research', in Marsden, T., Lowe, P. and Whatmore, S. (eds) *Rural Restructuring: Global Processes and their Responses*, London: David Fulton.

Reimer, B. (1986) 'Women as farm labour', *Rural Sociology*, 51(2), 143–55.

Repassy, H. (1991) 'Changing gender roles in Hungarian agriculture', *Journal of Rural Studies*, 7(1/2), 23–29.

Report of the Fourth Joint Committee on Women's Rights (1994) *Women and Rural Development*, Dublin: The Stationary Office.

Rossier, R. (1993) 'The farm woman's work today', Paper to 15th European Congress of Rural Sociology, Wageningen, The Netherlands.

Rottman, D. (1994) *Income Distribution within Irish Households*, Dublin: Combat Poverty Agency.

Rottman, D., Hannan, D., Hardiman, N. and Wiley, M. (1982) *The Distribution of Income in the Repubic of Ireland: A study in Social Class and Family-Cycle Inequalities*, Dublin: Economic and Social Research Institute.

Sachs, C.E. (1983) *The Invisible Farmers*, New Jersey: Rowman and Allanheld.

Salant, P. (1983) *Farm women: contribution to farm and family*, USDA Economic Research Service, Report No. 140.

Sargent, L. (ed.) (1991) *Women and Revolution: The Unhappy Marriage of Marxism and Feminism*, London: Pluto Press.

Scheper-Hughes, N. (1979) *Saints, Scholars and Schizophrenics: Mental Illness in Rural Ireland*, California: University of California Press.

Scully, J.J. (1971) *Agriculture in the West of Ireland*, Dublin: Stationary Office.

Seccombe, W. (1974) 'The housewife and her labour under capitalism', *New Left Review*, 83(1), 3–29.

Second Commission on the Status of Women (1993), *Report to Government*, Dublin: Government Publications.

Sheridan, R. (1982) 'Women's contribution to farming', *Farm and Food Research*, 13(2), 46–48.

Shortall, S. (1991) 'The dearth of data on Irish farm wives: a critical review of the literature', *The Economic and Social Review*, 22(4), 311–32.

Shortall, S. (1992) 'Power analysis and farm wives: an empirical analysis of the power relationships affecting women on Irish farms', *Sociologia Ruralis*, 32(4): 431–51.

Stacey, J. (1986) 'Are Feminists afraid to leave home? The challenge of conservative pro-family feminism', in Mitchell, J. and Oakley, A. (eds) *What is Feminism?* Oxford: Basil Blackwell.

Stanley, L. (1990) (ed.) *Feminist Praxis: Research, Theory and Epistemology in Feminist Sociology*, New York: Routledge.

Stanley, L. and Wise, S. (1983) *Breaking Out: Feminist Consciousness and Feminist Research*, London: Routledge and Kegan Paul.

Stratigaki, M. (1988) 'Agricultural modernisation and the gender division of labour: the case of Heraklion, Greece', *Sociologia Ruralis*, 23(4), 248–62.

Symes, D. (1972) 'Farm household and farm performance: a study of twentieth century changes in Ballyferriter, southwest Ireland', *Ethnology*, 11, 25–38.

Symes, D. (1991) 'Changing gender roles in productionist and post-productionist capitalist agriculture', *Journal of Rural Studies*, 7(1/2), 85–90.

Symes, D and Marsden, T. (1983) 'Complementary roles and asymmetrical lives: farmers' wives in a large farm environment', *Sociologia Ruralis*, 23(3/4), 229–41.

Teagasc (1991) *National Farm Survey 1990: Regional Results*, Dublin: Teagasc.

Thompson, L. (1992) 'Feminist methodology for family studies', *Journal of Marriage and the Family*, 54(1), 3–18.

Thompson, L. (1993) 'Conceptualizing gender in marriage: the case of marital care', *Journal of Marriage and the Family*, 55, 557–69.

Tovey, H. (1992) 'Rural sociology in Ireland: a review', *Irish Journal of Sociology*, 2, 96–121.

Travers, P. (1995) 'Emigration and gender: The case of Ireland 1922–60, in O'Dowd, M. and Wichert, S. *Chattel, Servant or Citizen: Women's Status in Church, State and Society*, Belfast: The Institute of Irish Studies, The Queen's University of Belfast.

Vandergeest, P. (1988) 'Commercialisation and commoditisation: a dialogue between perspectives', *Sociologia Ruralis*, 28(1), 7–29.

Vanek, J. (1980) 'Time spent in housework', in Amsden, A. (ed.) *The Economics of Women and Work*, Harmondsworth: Penguin.

Villarreal, M. (1992) 'The poverty of practice: power, gender and intervention from an actor-oriented perspective', in Long, N. and Long, A. (eds) *Battlefields of Knowledge*, London: Routledge.

Vries, W. M. de (1990) 'Pluriactivity and changing household relations in the Land van Mass en Waal, The Netherlands', *Journal of Rural Studies*, 6(4), 423–28.

Walby, S. (1990) *Theorizing Patriarchy*, Oxford: Basil Blackwell.

Waring, M. (1988) *If Women Counted: A New Feminist Economics*, London: Macmillan.

Whatmore, S.J., Munton, R.J., Little, J.K. and Marsden, T.K. (1986) 'Internal and external relations in the transformation of the farm family', *Sociologia Ruralis*, 26 (3/4), 396–98.

Whatmore, S.J., Munton, R.J., Marsden, T.K. and Little, J. K. (1987a) 'Towards a typology of farm businesses in contemporary British agriculture', *Sociologia Ruralis*, 27(1), 21–37.

Whatmore, S.J., Munton, R.J., Marsden, T.K. and Little, J. K. (1987b) 'Interpreting a relational typology of farm businesses in southern England', *Sociologia Ruralis*, 27(2/3), 103–22.

Whatmore, S. (1991) *Farming Women: Gender Work and Family Enterprise*, London: Macmillan.

Whelan, C.T., Breen, R. and Whelan, B. (1992) 'Industrialisation, class formation and social mobility in Ireland', in Goldthorpe, J.H. and Whelan, C.T. (eds) *The Development of Industrial Society in Ireland*, Oxford: Oxford University Press.

Whitehead, A. (1981) '"I'm hungry, mum", The politics of domestic budgeting', in Young, K., Wolkowitz, C. and McCullagh, R. (eds) *Of Marriage and the Market: Women's Subordination in International Perspective*, London: CSE Books.

Wilson, G. (1987) 'Money: patterns of responsibility and irresponsibility in marriage', in Brannen, J. and Wilson, G. (eds) *Give and Take in Families*, London: Allen and Unwin.

Wilson, G. (1991) 'Thoughts on the co-operative conflict model of the household in relation to economic method', *IDS Bulletin*, 22(1), 31–36.

INDEX